D0655158

EGMONT

We bring stories to life

First published in Great Britain 2017, by Egmont UK Limited
The Yellow Building, 1 Nicholas Road
London W11 4AN

Written by Craig Jelley
Additional material by Marsh Davies
Designed by Joe Bolder and Andrea Philpots
Illustrations by Ryan Marsh
Cover designed by John Stuckey
Production by Louis Harvey
Special thanks to Lydia Winters, Owen Jones, Junkboy,
Martin Johansson, Marsh Davies and Jesper Öqvist.

© 2017 Mojang AB and Mojang Synergies AB. MINECRAFT is a trademark or registered
trademark of Mojang Synergies AB.

All rights reserved.

MOJANG

ISBN 978 1 4052 8600 8

66831/1
Printed in Italy

ONLINE SAFETY FOR YOUNGER FANS

Spending time online is great fun! H
keep the ir

- Never give out you
- Never giv
- Never tell anybody
- Never tell anybody y
- Be aware that you must be 13 or c
site policy and ask a pare
- Always tell a parer

Stay safe online. Any website add
to print. However, Egmont is not re
aware that online content can be su
unsuitable for children. We advise

Coventry City Council	
COU	
3 8002 02347 058 8	
Askews & Holts	Sep-2017
J794.8 JUNIOR NON-FI	£9.99

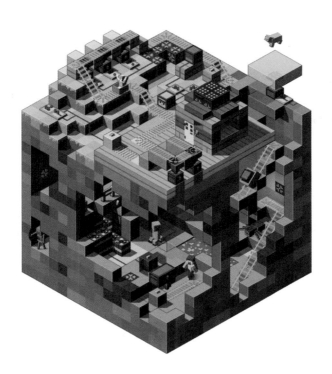

GUIDE TO:

◆REDSTONE

CONTENTS

INTRODUCTION

Welcome to our Guide to Redstone – Minecraft's answer to electronics! Lay down redstone dust like electrical wire, add a few simple components, and you can build clever computers or crafty combination locks, trigger human catapults or trap mischievous mobs. It's powerful and versatile! So versatile, in fact, that we're often gobsmacked by the stuff the community makes – everything from pixel-art editors to massive walking mechs. We hope this guide gives you the know-how to unleash your imagination and build the next thing that leaves us gawping!

MARSH DAVIES
THE MOJANG TEAM

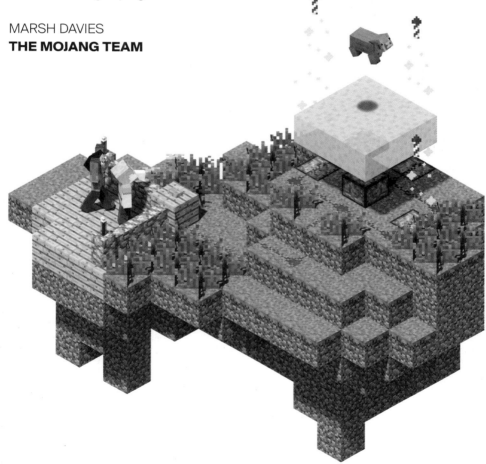

THE BASICS

Before we start building incredible contraptions, we're going to look at the different redstone components, what they do and how we can use them in simple creations that you can build straight away. Learning the basics first will ensure you become a true redstone expert, capable of building awesome mechanisms.

FINDING REDSTONE

Redstone is a mysterious substance that is used to power mechanisms and traps. In its rawest form, it's an ore found underground, but it can be mined and refined into redstone dust. As well as forming the basis for redstone circuits, it's also an important crafting ingredient for redstone components.

REDSTONE LOCATIONS

When hunting for redstone, you'll want to focus on certain Overworld locations. Let's take a look at where redstone naturally occurs.

REDSTONE ORE

REDSTONE DUST

1 Redstone dust can be found in woodland mansions, though the deadly illagers protect the chests in which it is found.

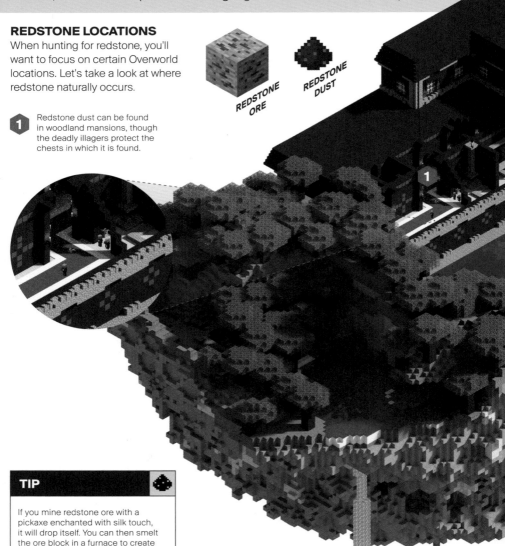

TIP

If you mine redstone ore with a pickaxe enchanted with silk touch, it will drop itself. You can then smelt the ore block in a furnace to create redstone dust.

2 When defeated, witches will drop stacks of up to six pieces of redstone. Hunt them down in swamp biomes.

3 Redstone dust can be found in chests in other naturally generated structures too – dungeons, strongholds and abandoned mineshafts will all have some.

4 Redstone ore generates naturally underground, within 1 to 16 blocks from the bedrock layer. When mined, the ore will drop 4-5 redstone dusts.

REDSTONE DUST

So what does redstone dust actually do? Well, it has the ability to transmit a redstone signal from a power source to a redstone component, allowing for an almost infinite number of possible mechanisms and circuits. It's really very useful!

When placed, redstone dust lies flat on the ground and is initially dark red in colour. When it's activated, it will glow a bright red and emit particles. When powered, the redstone signal will travel a maximum of 15 blocks, unless it is powered again along the way.

DEACTIVATED

ACTIVATED

REDSTONE DUST BEHAVIOUR

In its most basic behaviour, redstone will interact with redstone in adjacent blocks, stretching out and connecting with it.

If the redstone is placed beside an existing line of redstone, then it will curve sideways, creating a turn in the circuit.

If redstone is placed on both sides of an existing line then it will fork in multiple directions, which can split a redstone signal.

A split signal can be brought back around and joined together again with more redstone dust, creating a signal loop.

Additional redstone can be placed inside a loop to create a grid, which can be used to power a group of blocks simultaneously.

Redstone can link with redstone placed a level higher or lower. It can also form loops, curves and grids with redstone on other levels.

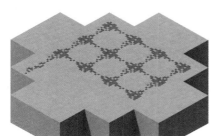

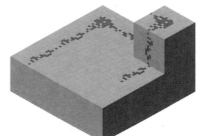

TICKS AND TIMING

Time passing in Minecraft is measured as 'ticks' and there are 20 ticks per second. Redstone signals are measured in the same way. You'll see the term 'redstone tick', or just 'tick', a lot in this book – each redstone tick is the length of two game ticks, meaning there are 10 redstone ticks per second. You don't need to know too much about how or why it works, but the lower the number of ticks, the faster a redstone signal will travel.

POWER AND STRENGTH

Sometimes we'll refer to strength of redstone signals in this book. The strength ranges from 1 (lowest) to 15 (highest). The signal strength can depend on the power source that is being used. You'll see a lot more later on in the book about how power sources produce different signal strengths, and how the signal strength can be altered.

REDSTONE POWER SOURCES

There are lots of ways to power a circuit. Each power source offers a different combination of signal strength and interaction with other redstone components. Let's take a look at your options so you can decide which is right for your build.

MANUAL ACTIVATORS

The simplest power sources in Minecraft are buttons and levers, easily crafted from wood or stone. They will need to be manually activated by a player, and, even at this simple level, have different characteristics that make them more appropriate for certain build types.

Here we see the button in its simplest usage. Placed beside an iron door, the button will send power through the solid block it's placed on when pushed, opening the door for a brief time.

BUTTON

Buttons are crafted from a single block of stone or wood planks. When pushed they provide a temporary redstone signal at maximum strength. They can be placed on any side of a solid block, including the top and bottom.

BUTTON RECIPE

LEVER

Crafted by combining a stick and cobblestone, levers also produce the maximum redstone signal. However, unlike buttons, they are switchable sources, which means that the redstone signal will toggle on and off each time it is used.

LEVER RECIPE

In this example, the lever will open up the trapdoor on the adjacent block when interacted with once. It will stay open until the lever is activated once again.

TRAP ACTIVATORS

These power sources are perfect for players who like to build sneaky traps. Most of them look innocent enough, or can't be seen at all, which is why they're so perfect. Your target won't know they've activated a cunning contraption until it's too late.

PRESSURE PLATES

Pressure plates can be made with wood or stone, and are often used in simple, non-trap builds too. Each sends a temporary redstone signal at the maximum strength through solid blocks or redstone components. They can be activated by players or mobs stepping on them, however, the wooden pressure plate will also produce an output when an item is dropped on it.

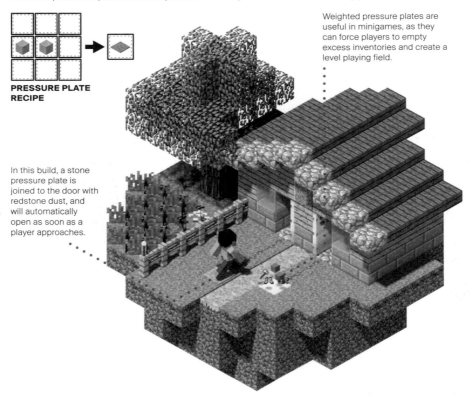

PRESSURE PLATE RECIPE

Weighted pressure plates are useful in minigames, as they can force players to empty excess inventories and create a level playing field.

In this build, a stone pressure plate is joined to the door with redstone dust, and will automatically open as soon as a player approaches.

WEIGHTED PRESSURE PLATES

Weighted pressure plates come in a light variety (made with gold ingots), and heavy variety (made with iron ingots). The signal strength they produce depends on the number of 'entities' on them (this includes players, mobs and dropped items). The light plate requires 57 items to create maximum signal strength, whereas at least 598 are needed to do the same with the heavy variety.

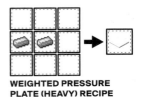

WEIGHTED PRESSURE PLATE (HEAVY) RECIPE

TRIPWIRE

The nearly-invisible tripwire is a particularly crafty way to activate a trap. Tripwire hooks need to be attached together by string, but can be placed up to 40 blocks apart. When the tripwire is broken by a mob or player, each hook will output a maximum signal to adjacent blocks.

Tripwires won't break when activated, so players and mobs will repeatedly activate them. This makes it perfect for a security system – link it up to redstone lamps to get notified whenever someone enters your HQ.

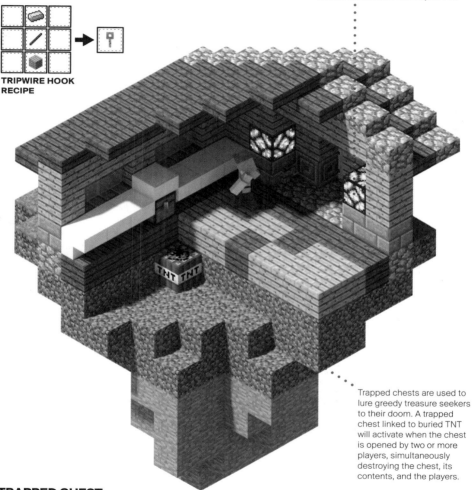

TRIPWIRE HOOK RECIPE

Trapped chests are used to lure greedy treasure seekers to their doom. A trapped chest linked to buried TNT will activate when the chest is opened by two or more players, simultaneously destroying the chest, its contents, and the players.

TRAPPED CHEST

The trapped chest is almost indistinguishable from its regular counterpart, except for a red band around the clasp. They can be used for regular storage, as long as any redstone traps are disabled before opening. The output depends on how many people are viewing the chest's contents – the more people trying to steal from the trapped chest, the more powerful the signal.

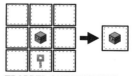

TRAPPED CHEST RECIPE

CONSTANT ACTIVATORS

In some situations you'll want a constant power source that doesn't require any interaction to generate a signal. This is where constant activators come in handy – they are permanently on, or alter their output depending on other external factors. Here's a guide to using them effectively.

REDSTONE TORCH

As well as being a source of light, redstone torches also provide a maximum redstone signal of 15. Redstone torches can be inverted in redstone circuits, so that they are constantly off rather than on.

Placing another redstone torch under the first will invert the signal and turn off the first redstone torch. They can also be placed on the side of blocks, to provide power through solid blocks above, and redstone components on horizontally adjacent blocks.

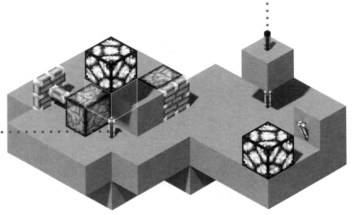

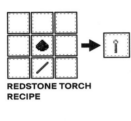

REDSTONE TORCH RECIPE

This build shows the behaviour of a redstone signal from a redstone torch. It can travel upwards through a solid block, or power redstone components directly beside it, however, it won't travel through a solid block beside it.

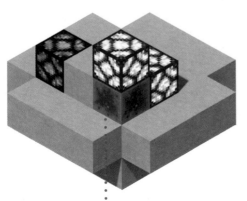

REDSTONE BLOCK

Redstone blocks are made from, and can produce, nine pieces of redstone dust, which makes them great for storing excess redstone. When placed, they can power redstone components on adjacent blocks in all directions, as well as mechanisms like doors and pistons.

The redstone block consistently powers two redstone lamps, one to the side and one above. The redstone block won't provide power through adjacent solid blocks, and it will also deactivate other power sources like the redstone torch.

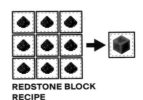

REDSTONE BLOCK RECIPE

DAYLIGHT SENSOR

Daylight sensors produce different levels of power depending on the sunlight in the world – more when it's daytime, less at night, though weather also has an effect. They can also be inverted by interacting with the block, so that they produce more power when the world is darker.

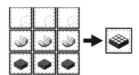

DAYLIGHT SENSOR RECIPE

Daylight sensors are handy for creating automatic lighting systems. This room has two daylight sensors on the roof, one regular and one inverted, which are linked to redstone lamps beneath. At least one of the lamps will be on at any point during the day.

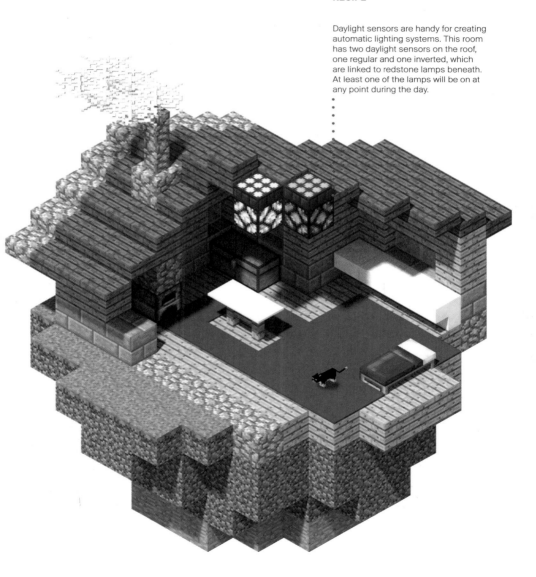

OBSERVERS

The observer block is the newest addition to the redstone repertoire, and produces a signal when it detects an update in the block it's monitoring. It can fully replace a BUD (block-update detection) circuit, which is quite complex and detects a more exclusive range of updates.

BLOCK FACES

The observer has two functional faces – the observer face, which monitors the block directly ahead, and an output face, which produces the redstone signal in the opposite direction. Observers can be placed to monitor blocks in all directions.

The observer is made from cobblestone, redstone dust and Nether quartz. It's not affected by external redstone sources, so it can't be inverted as redstone torches can. When activated, the observer will output the maximum redstone signal too.

OBSERVER FACE   **OUTPUT FACE**

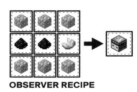

OBSERVER RECIPE

DETECTION VARIETY

So what exactly can an observer block detect? Among other things, it will observe the activation of powered rails, pistons extending, and the spreading of grass to dirt (and vice-versa). In this example, when the daylight sensor inverts or senses a change in light, the observer will detect it and power the circuit, activating a sound from the note block.

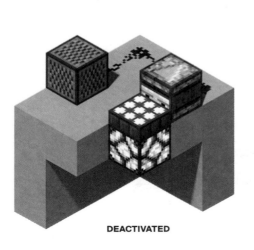
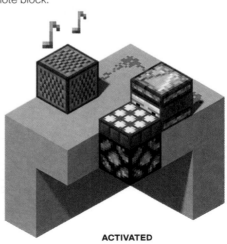

DEACTIVATED   **ACTIVATED**

UPDATING OBSERVERS

Observers can also be moved within a circuit. When they're pushed or pulled by a piston, this will also count as a block update, but it will only output a signal when it reaches its new position.

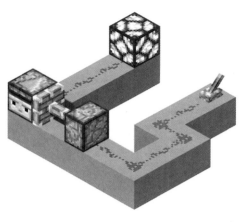

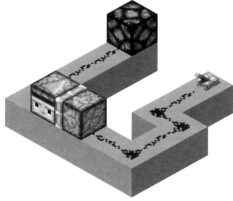

BUD CIRCUIT

For those block updates that an observer isn't capable of detecting, you'll need to use a BUD circuit instead. Among other things, it can detect a furnace beginning to smelt, changes in redstone power levels, and the placement or removal of blocks, like the crafting table that's been added in the examples below.

MOJANG STUFF

BUD circuits work by exploiting a bug – often called 'quasi-connectivity' by the community – which became so useful to crafters that we made it a feature!

MANIPULATION

We've seen that there are plenty of ways to power a circuit and provide it with a signal, but that's just the beginning of what you can do with redstone. The blocks that we'll look at in this section manipulate the strength and flow of the signal, set the speed that it travels at, and even influence non-redstone elements.

REDSTONE REPEATERS

You've learnt how to power circuits using different power sources, so let's look at how you can use blocks to adapt circuits to suit your needs. The first block you'll need is the redstone repeater, which is shown to the right.

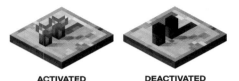

ACTIVATED   **DEACTIVATED**

REPEATER FUNCTIONS

1

Repeaters can amplify redstone signals back up to full strength.

2

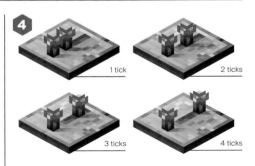

Repeaters can combine with other repeaters to create 'locks' in circuits.

3

Repeaters ensure signals only move one way through a circuit.

4

1 tick   2 ticks

3 ticks   4 ticks

Repeaters can delay signals by 1-4 ticks depending on the chosen setting.

HOW REPEATERS ARE USED

Let's explore how each of these functions can be applied to help create a variety of circuits that perform different tasks. You'll see as we go through the book how repeater functions are used in actual contraptions.

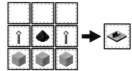

REDSTONE REPEATER RECIPE

AMPLIFICATION

Place a repeater on the fifteenth block of a circuit, when the redstone signal is down to its • • • • • • • • • • • • • • lowest strength (1), and it will amplify the signal back up to its maximum strength (15).

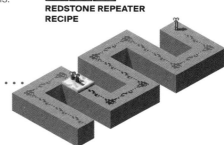

LOCK FUNCTION

Both lamps are powered by the same lever. When one of the side-facing repeaters is powered by • • • • • • • • • • • • • • the lever on the left, it locks one repeater and blocks the signal reaching the redstone lamp.

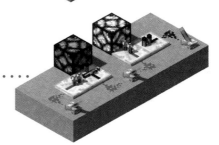

ONE-WAY MOVEMENT

When the circuit is active and the lever is pulled, a signal remains in the left of the circuit. This causes • • • • • • • • • • • • • • • the piston to pull the other piston back. The repeaters stop the signal reaching the right of the circuit.

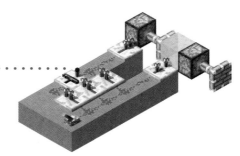

DELAY FUNCTION

When the lever is pulled, the lamp on the right lights up first. The circuit leading to the lamp • • • • • • • • • • • • • on the left has a repeater set to 4 ticks, delaying the signal and creating a staggered activation.

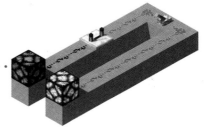

REDSTONE COMPARATORS

A redstone comparator is a component that compares up to three redstone signals and outputs a signal accordingly. You'll see it has three redstone torches on top of the block and an arrow facing in the output direction. The torches at the back of the block indicate if it is outputting a signal, and the front torch indicates which 'mode' it's in.

The comparator has two modes, which can be changed by interacting with it. This will turn the front torch on and off – if it's off, the comparator is in 'comparison mode', which compares a signal from the back to the side inputs. If the torch is on, then the comparator is in 'subtraction mode', which means that the side inputs are subtracted from the strength of the rear input.

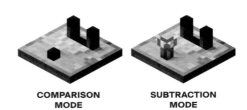

COMPARISON MODE   **SUBTRACTION MODE**

COMPARATOR FUNCTIONS

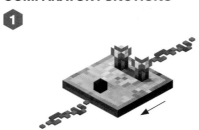

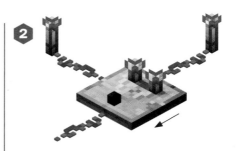

A comparator sustains a signal flowing into it, and outputs a signal of the same strength.

A comparator compares a signal going through the rear input to a signal going into the side.

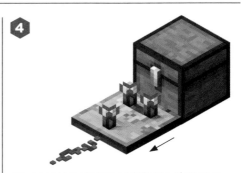

In subtraction mode, comparators output a signal equal to the rear input minus side input.

Comparators detect the fullness of storage items and output a corresponding signal.

HOW COMPARATORS ARE USED

The comparator is just as useful and versatile as the redstone repeater. Here are some examples to show each of its functions in action. You'll see more of how the comparator's functions work in later builds too.

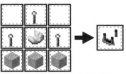

REDSTONE COMPARATOR RECIPE

 MAINTAINING A SIGNAL

The comparator and a repeater are in the same position in parallel circuit strands. The comparator doesn't increase the signal, which limits the signal's reach, so the redstone lamp on its strand is off.

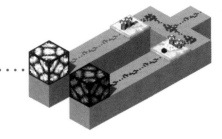

 COMPARING SIGNALS

If the signal entering the side of the comparator is weaker than the one entering the rear, then the signal is maintained and output through the front. If the side input is stronger when compared, there will be no output. It can compare up to two inputs, one entering each side of the comparator.

Side input stronger

Side input weaker

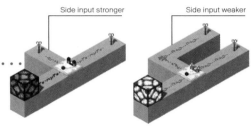

 SUBTRACTING SIGNALS

When switched to subtraction mode, the strength of the side signal is subtracted from the rear signal, and a reduced redstone signal is output, which leaves the redstone lamp deactivated. It can subtract up to two inputs, one from each side of the comparator.

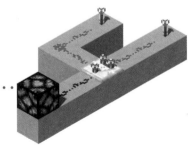

 MEASURING STORAGE

Comparators in these circuits measure how much is in each of the chests. When completely full with stacks of 64 items, comparators output a maximum strength signal, when empty they won't output a signal at all.

Full

Half-full

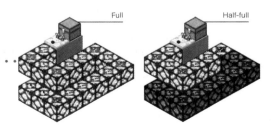

PISTONS, STICKY PISTONS AND SLIME BLOCKS

Now that you've grasped the basics of redstone circuitry, we can take a look at how circuits can be used to physically move blocks around. With the help of pistons and slime blocks, your circuits are able to push, pull, drag, break and even bounce blocks.

PISTON

The primary function of the piston is to physically move blocks around in a circuit. When powered, the head of the piston extends to push a block directly in front of it by a single block space. When the signal stops, the head retracts back to its original position.

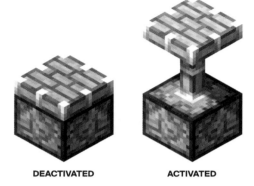

DEACTIVATED   **ACTIVATED**

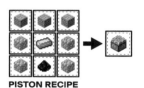

PISTON RECIPE

STICKY PISTON

Pistons are able to push a maximum of 12 blocks at a time. Sticky pistons are even more useful – they stick to blocks when extended, and pull them backwards when they retract. This is shown in action below.

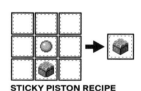

STICKY PISTON RECIPE

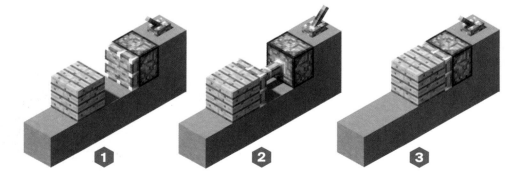

SLIME BLOCK

Crafted from slimeballs, slime blocks can be used in circuits to grab and move blocks. They're treated as a transparent block as they let light through, but, unlike most transparent blocks, you can also place blocks on them.

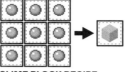

SLIME BLOCK RECIPE

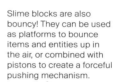

Slime blocks are also bouncy! They can be used as platforms to bounce items and entities up in the air, or combined with pistons to create a forceful pushing mechanism.

The slime block's sticky quality allows it to pick up adjacent blocks, and push or pull them providing there are no more than 12. Because it can pick up blocks in all directions, a slime block attached to a piston allows a lot more possibilities than sticky pistons.

OBSIDIAN

There are some blocks in Minecraft that have extremely high blast resistance and others that are completely immovable by pistons or slime blocks. Obsidian possesses both of these qualities, which makes it an incredibly handy tool for your redstone arsenal.

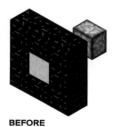

BEFORE

AFTER

BEFORE

AFTER

Obsidian is particularly useful when you're creating redstone contraptions in which slime blocks or sticky pistons are in danger of moving critical parts of the redstone circuit. The images above show what happens when you use obsidian instead of clay with a sticky slime block.

SECRET PISTON PASSAGE

We've discovered quite a few redstone components so far, so now we're going to create our first simple build – a secret passage that's cleverly activated by sticky pistons. It can be used to hide an entrance to a treasure stash or perhaps a top secret mine.

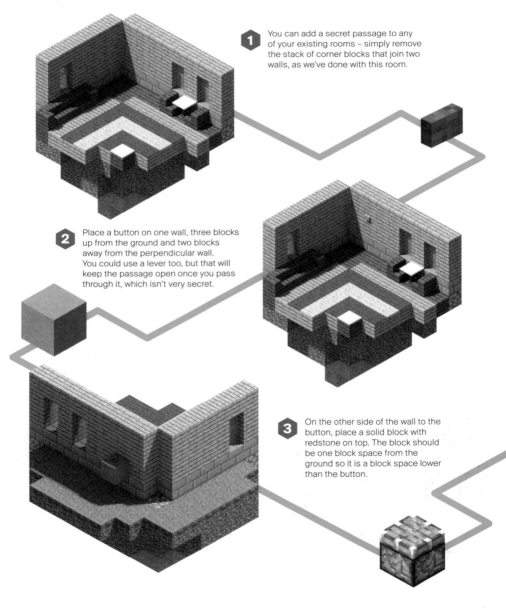

1 You can add a secret passage to any of your existing rooms – simply remove the stack of corner blocks that join two walls, as we've done with this room.

2 Place a button on one wall, three blocks up from the ground and two blocks away from the perpendicular wall. You could use a lever too, but that will keep the passage open once you pass through it, which isn't very secret.

3 On the other side of the wall to the button, place a solid block with redstone on top. The block should be one block space from the ground so it is a block space lower than the button.

6 Now you know where the entrance will appear, you can add a secret passage leading to other rooms, hidden floors, or emergency escape routes under your building.

5 That's the mechanism completed! When you press the button, it will activate the redstone dust behind the wall, which in turn inverts the redstone torch and deactivates the piston. This pulls the wall blocks back and reveals the passage.

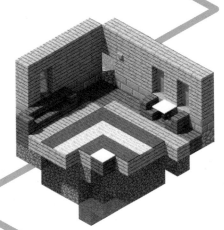

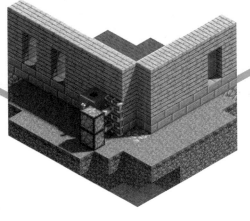

4 Place a redstone torch on the front of the solid block, then stack two sticky pistons beside it, facing the wall, one on top of the other. The sticky pistons will instantly activate and extend to touch the wall.

OUTPUT

So we can power redstone circuits and we can control what they do, now it's time to look at what they can produce. Many functions of pistons can be considered output, but there are some blocks that specialise in the effects that they can produce, which we'll look at in this section.

DISPENSERS, DROPPERS AND HOPPERS

The first output group contains dispensers, droppers and hoppers. All of them contain storage for items, and have the ability to move those items in different ways and for different purposes.

DISPENSERS

Dispensers are created with cobblestone, bows and redstone dust, and are able to produce an output facing any direction. They can hold nine stacks of items and will eject an item, sometimes activated, when powered.

Dispensers activate once after a two-tick delay, so would need to be repeatedly activated, manually or in a circuit, to create repetition. It also has a tick delay on reactivation, so rapid output isn't easy to achieve.

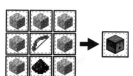

DISPENSER RECIPE

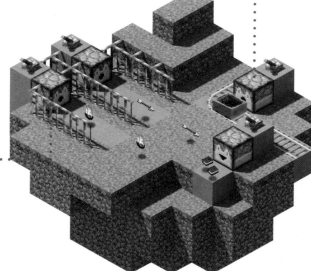

Dispensers can be used to fire arrows and fireballs using fire charges, deploy minecarts to rails, and place blocks like jack o'lanterns.

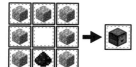

DROPPER RECIPE

DROPPERS

The dropper is so called as it performs a similar function to dropping items from your inventory. Unlike dispensers, it can't activate items, but merely throws them forward.

Both the dispenser and the dropper have a special interface for storing items. Each has nine slots to put items in, but no way of selecting a slot to output. If there are multiple item types in the slots, a random item will be chosen to output. Hoppers have just five storage slots instead of nine.

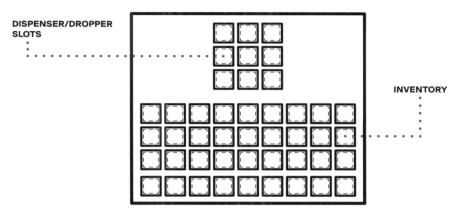

DISPENSER/DROPPER SLOTS

INVENTORY

HOPPERS

Hoppers are more similar to droppers as they also only have the ability to move items. The hopper has a unique function that can be used to siphon items from one object to another. This can be used to collect drops from a mob-infested cave, or move items from one chest to another.

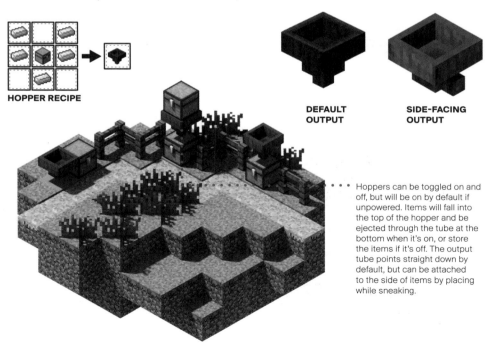

HOPPER RECIPE

DEFAULT OUTPUT

SIDE-FACING OUTPUT

Hoppers can be toggled on and off, but will be on by default if unpowered. Items will fall into the top of the hopper and be ejected through the tube at the bottom when it's on, or store the items if it's off. The output tube points straight down by default, but can be attached to the side of items by placing while sneaking.

AUTOMATIC FIREWORK DISPLAY

We're going to use our new-found knowledge of dispensers to create an awesome automatic firework display. This build also utilises repeaters to cause a delayed redstone signal to certain dispensers so it creates staggered explosions in the display.

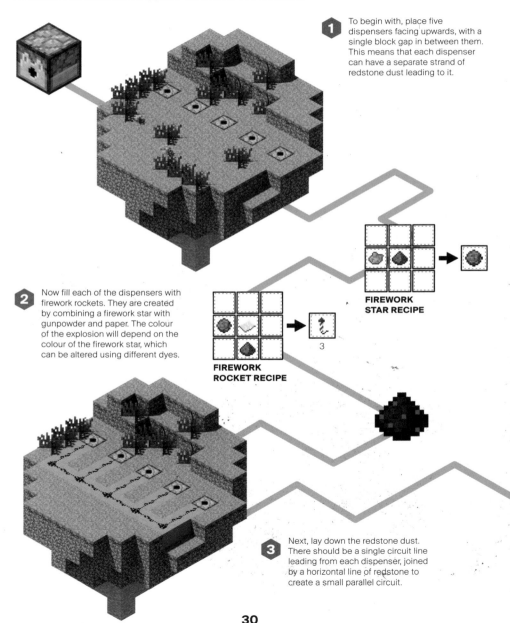

1 To begin with, place five dispensers facing upwards, with a single block gap in between them. This means that each dispenser can have a separate strand of redstone dust leading to it.

FIREWORK STAR RECIPE

2 Now fill each of the dispensers with firework rockets. They are created by combining a firework star with gunpowder and paper. The colour of the explosion will depend on the colour of the firework star, which can be altered using different dyes.

FIREWORK ROCKET RECIPE

3

3 Next, lay down the redstone dust. There should be a single circuit line leading from each dispenser, joined by a horizontal line of redstone to create a small parallel circuit.

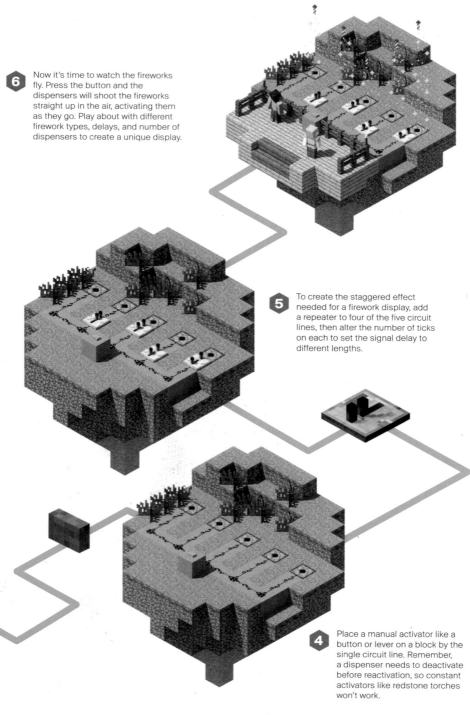

6 Now it's time to watch the fireworks fly. Press the button and the dispensers will shoot the fireworks straight up in the air, activating them as they go. Play about with different firework types, delays, and number of dispensers to create a unique display.

5 To create the staggered effect needed for a firework display, add a repeater to four of the five circuit lines, then alter the number of ticks on each to set the signal delay to different lengths.

4 Place a manual activator like a button or lever on a block by the single circuit line. Remember, a dispenser needs to deactivate before reactivation, so constant activators like redstone torches won't work.

ACTIVATOR, POWERED AND DETECTOR RAILS

There are a number of specialised redstone rails in Minecraft that can work as part of a circuit. These cross the spectrum of functions that we've already seen – they can output power, and detect storage, while others still will interact with a minecart that passes over the rail.

DETECTOR RAIL

Detector rails work in a similar way to pressure plates – they detect when a minecart passes over them, and output a full redstone signal to adjacent blocks and components.

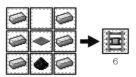

DETECTOR RAIL RECIPE

POWERED RAIL

Powered rails accelerate minecarts along a route. They require a redstone signal to provide the boost, otherwise they may actually slow down minecarts. Activated powered rails will conduct a signal to eight adjacent powered rails.

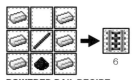

POWERED RAIL RECIPE

 Detector and powered rails can be used to provide continuous momentum along a track. By placing a detector rail in front of a powered rail, passing carts will activate a boost. If this is done all along a track, then movement should be continuous.

Combined with comparators, detector rails can measure how full minecarts with hoppers or chests are, and output a corresponding signal. If storage is full, the signal will be at its maximum, but if it's almost empty, it will only produce a weak signal.

ACTIVATOR RAIL

The final redstone rail is the activator rail. It can be powered by the detector rail or any other redstone power source and has a number of functions, which depend on its activation state and the type of minecart that is passing over it.

ACTIVATOR RAIL RECIPE

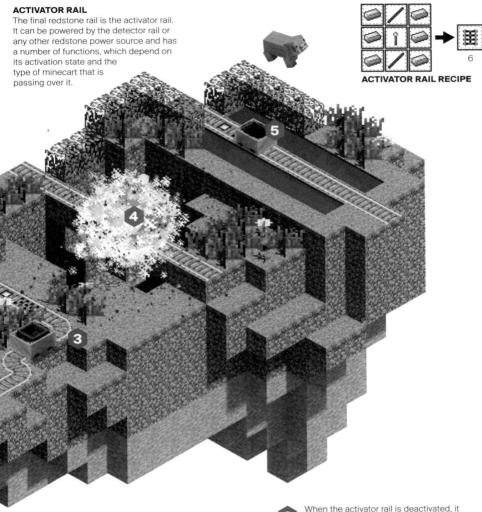

3 When the activator rail is deactivated, it can activate a minecart with a hopper, allowing it to pick up items along its route, until it is full or deactivated. Conversely, when it's activated it will deactivate the same minecart, stopping it from collecting items.

4 Activator rails can also begin the detonation of a minecart with TNT. This is particularly useful for mining as all rails are immune to the blast. This makes it easy to send multiple TNT minecarts in quick succession to mine a large area.

5 The final activator rail function can be seen when an entity in a minecart passes over the activator rail. The activator rail will eject the mob or player in the cart!

TIP

Redstone-enabled rails are unable to curve like normal rails. They must be used as straight track.

REDSTONE INTERSECTION

Building a working redstone rail system makes it much easier to travel across the vast expanse of your world. This redstone intersection will give you complete control over your route and allow you to change your intended direction without ever leaving your minecart.

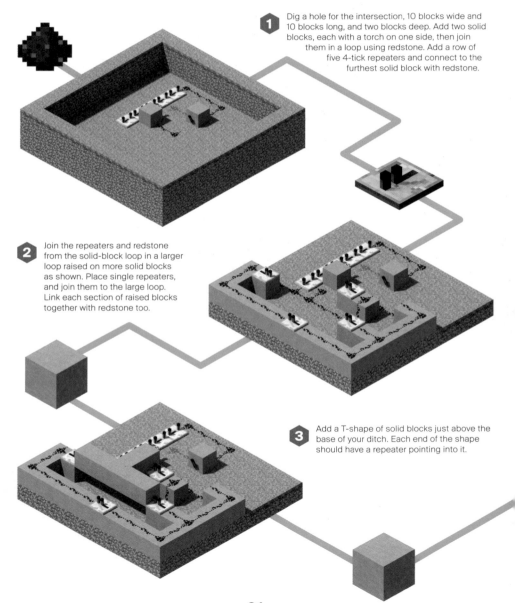

1 Dig a hole for the intersection, 10 blocks wide and 10 blocks long, and two blocks deep. Add two solid blocks, each with a torch on one side, then join them in a loop using redstone. Add a row of five 4-tick repeaters and connect to the furthest solid block with redstone.

2 Join the repeaters and redstone from the solid-block loop in a larger loop raised on more solid blocks as shown. Place single repeaters, and join them to the large loop. Link each section of raised blocks together with redstone too.

3 Add a T-shape of solid blocks just above the base of your ditch. Each end of the shape should have a repeater pointing into it.

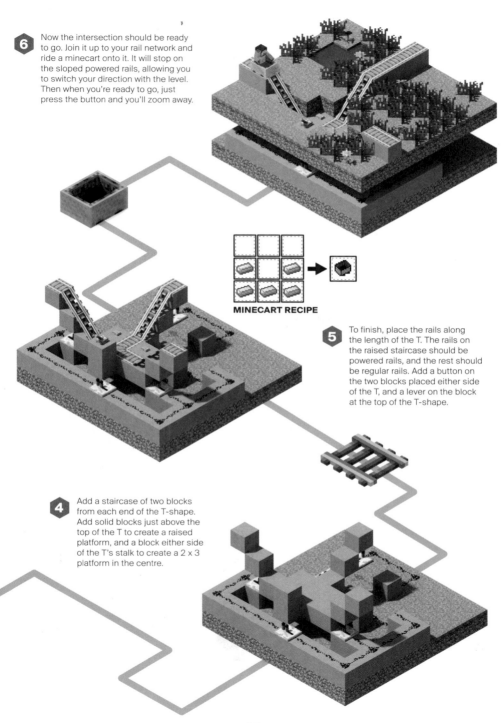

6 Now the intersection should be ready to go. Join it up to your rail network and ride a minecart onto it. It will stop on the sloped powered rails, allowing you to switch your direction with the level. Then when you're ready to go, just press the button and you'll zoom away.

MINECART RECIPE

5 To finish, place the rails along the length of the T. The rails on the raised staircase should be powered rails, and the rest should be regular rails. Add a button on the two blocks placed either side of the T, and a lever on the block at the top of the T-shape.

4 Add a staircase of two blocks from each end of the T-shape. Add solid blocks just above the top of the T to create a raised platform, and a block either side of the T's stalk to create a 2 x 3 platform in the centre.

NOTE BLOCK AND REDSTONE LAMPS

The final redstone output components are the ones that produce light and sound. Note blocks can play different types of sound at different pitches, while redstone lamps are similar in appearance to glowstone, though they have the advantage of being switchable.

NOTE BLOCK

Each note block can be made with wood planks of any sort and a single piece of redstone dust. When a redstone signal passes through them they will produce a sound dependent on the block that it is standing on. The diagram below shows the block needed to produce each sound.

NOTE BLOCK RECIPE

The depth of customisation, along with a simple redstone circuit can be used to create everything from nursery rhymes to versions of popular songs. You can use repeater delays to create the correct rhythm of songs too.

The spectrum of a note block covers two octaves, which is a total of 24 notes. To tune your note blocks, simply interact with the block to raise the pitch by one note.

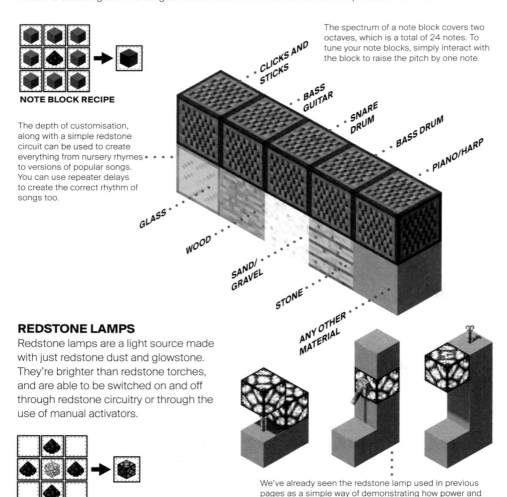

CLICKS AND STICKS

BASS GUITAR

SNARE DRUM

BASS DRUM

PIANO/HARP

GLASS

WOOD

SAND/ GRAVEL

STONE

ANY OTHER MATERIAL

REDSTONE LAMPS

Redstone lamps are a light source made with just redstone dust and glowstone. They're brighter than redstone torches, and are able to be switched on and off through redstone circuitry or through the use of manual activators.

REDSTONE LAMP RECIPE

We've already seen the redstone lamp used in previous pages as a simple way of demonstrating how power and manipulation blocks work. It can be powered from all sides so it is versatile enough to be used in walls, floors, ceilings, and specialised lighting objects.

SECURITY LOOP

Note blocks and redstone lamps serve a useful function as alert items. This build incorporates both types of items to create sound and lights that trigger when an intruder enters a building.

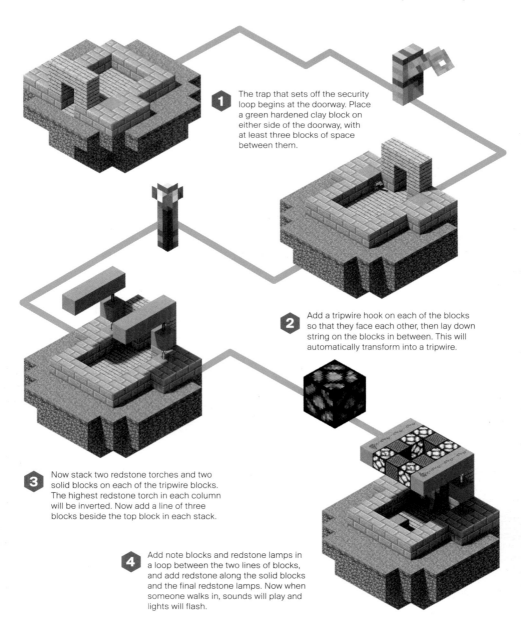

1 The trap that sets off the security loop begins at the doorway. Place a green hardened clay block on either side of the doorway, with at least three blocks of space between them.

2 Add a tripwire hook on each of the blocks so that they face each other, then lay down string on the blocks in between. This will automatically transform into a tripwire.

3 Now stack two redstone torches and two solid blocks on each of the tripwire blocks. The highest redstone torch in each column will be inverted. Now add a line of three blocks beside the top block in each stack.

4 Add note blocks and redstone lamps in a loop between the two lines of blocks, and add redstone along the solid blocks and the final redstone lamps. Now when someone walks in, sounds will play and lights will flash.

2

SIMPLE CIRCUITS

Now we have all the tools and redstone knowledge we need to progress to creating circuits. The circuits featured in this section are some of the easiest you can make, but you'll see from the example builds that it only takes a simple circuit to create a really cool mechanism.

CLOCK CIRCUITS

We're going to start off with the simplest circuit we can make – the clock circuit. Clock circuits conduct a signal that repeatedly triggers and travels through all the components, creating an infinite loop of activation for any attached mechanisms.

CLOCK CREATION

There are numerous ways to create a clock circuit, and even more ways that we can change its behaviour. On this spread we're going to look at types we can create with different components, so you can choose the one that's easiest for you.

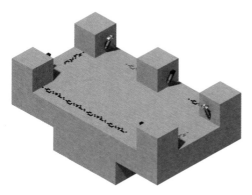

TORCH CLOCK

The simplest clock circuit utilises redstone torches. It requires an odd number of torches, and uses their ability to invert to repeatedly turn sections on and off. The torch clock above shows a 5-tick clock, which is the shortest stable clock that can be made, and takes 5 redstone ticks for the signal to loop.

REPEATER CLOCK

Repeater clocks are common as it's easy to amend the delay on redstone repeaters, and they can be rapid. This repeater clock is a 1-tick version, with no delay on the repeaters, which face alternate directions. The only thing to remember is to place the torch last, otherwise the signal will get stuck and stay on constantly.

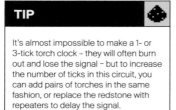

TIP ♣

It's almost impossible to make a 1- or 3-tick torch clock – they will often burn out and lose the signal – but to increase the number of ticks in this circuit, you can add pairs of torches in the same fashion, or replace the redstone with repeaters to delay the signal.

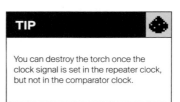

TIP ♣

You can destroy the torch once the clock signal is set in the repeater clock, but not in the comparator clock.

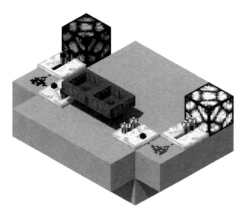

COMPARATOR CLOCK

Comparator clocks use a comparator set to subtraction mode to repeat a signal. It faces a solid block, from which redstone dust loops into the side of the comparator via a repeater, so the redstone doesn't join. The redstone torch behind the comparator provides a signal of 15, so when the side input is subtracted, it still results in an output and a repeating loop.

HOPPER CLOCK

Each hopper's output tube faces the other to create an alternating clock. Placing an item in one hopper will cause it to be passed back and forth indefinitely. The comparator beside each hopper measures the storage of each, which alternates between zero and one item, causing a small redstone signal output, which is then amplified by the repeater.

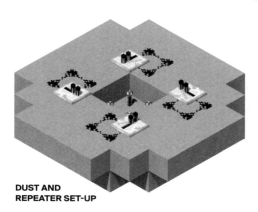

**DUST AND
REPEATER SET-UP**

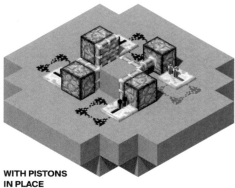

**WITH PISTONS
IN PLACE**

PISTON CLOCK

Unlike the other clock circuits, piston clocks have the advantage of being switchable, so they will only trigger when you want them to. This clock uses pistons to push a block around, which the redstone torches will pass a signal through, powering one of the four outer loops in turn.

MOB FARM TRAP

We're going to use the piston clock circuit as the basis for a handy mob farm, which lures in sunlight-hating mobs. It uses some of the outer loops of the piston clock to initiate different parts of the trap, and collect all the drops in easily accessible chests.

YOU WILL NEED:

138	16	12	20	65	8	4	7	4	4

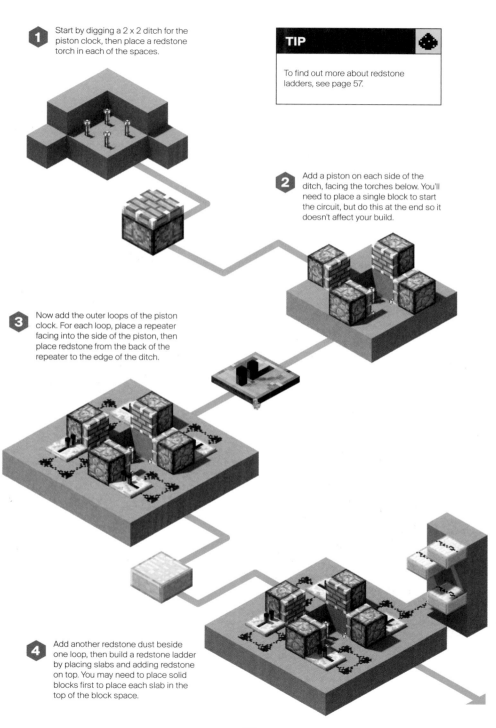

1. Start by digging a 2 x 2 ditch for the piston clock, then place a redstone torch in each of the spaces.

TIP

To find out more about redstone ladders, see page 57.

2. Add a piston on each side of the ditch, facing the torches below. You'll need to place a single block to start the circuit, but do this at the end so it doesn't affect your build.

3. Now add the outer loops of the piston clock. For each loop, place a repeater facing into the side of the piston, then place redstone from the back of the repeater to the edge of the ditch.

4. Add another redstone dust beside one loop, then build a redstone ladder by placing slabs and adding redstone on top. You may need to place solid blocks first to place each slab in the top of the block space.

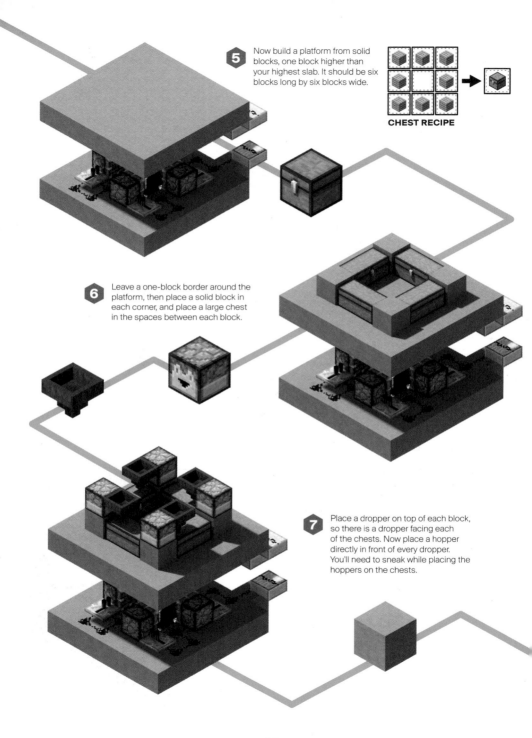

5 Now build a platform from solid blocks, one block higher than your highest slab. It should be six blocks long by six blocks wide.

CHEST RECIPE

6 Leave a one-block border around the platform, then place a solid block in each corner, and place a large chest in the spaces between each block.

7 Place a dropper on top of each block, so there is a dropper facing each of the chests. Now place a hopper directly in front of every dropper. You'll need to sneak while placing the hoppers on the chests.

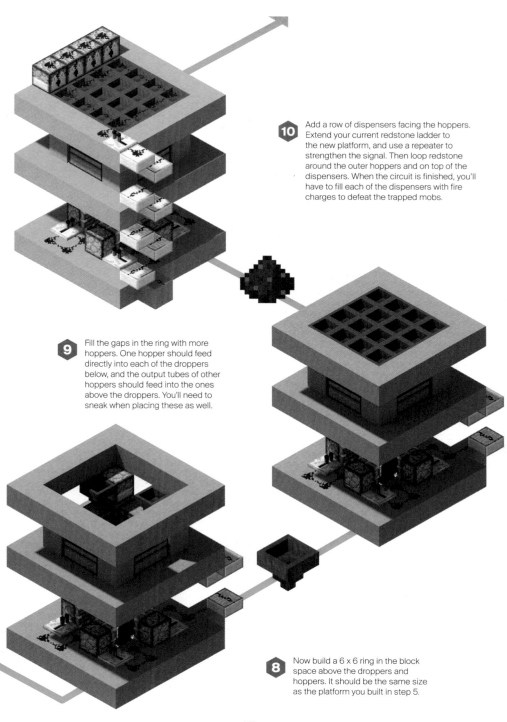

10 Add a row of dispensers facing the hoppers. Extend your current redstone ladder to the new platform, and use a repeater to strengthen the signal. Then loop redstone around the outer hoppers and on top of the dispensers. When the circuit is finished, you'll have to fill each of the dispensers with fire charges to defeat the trapped mobs.

9 Fill the gaps in the ring with more hoppers. One hopper should feed directly into each of the droppers below, and the output tubes of other hoppers should feed into the ones above the droppers. You'll need to sneak when placing these as well.

8 Now build a 6 x 6 ring in the block space above the droppers and hoppers. It should be the same size as the platform you built in step 5.

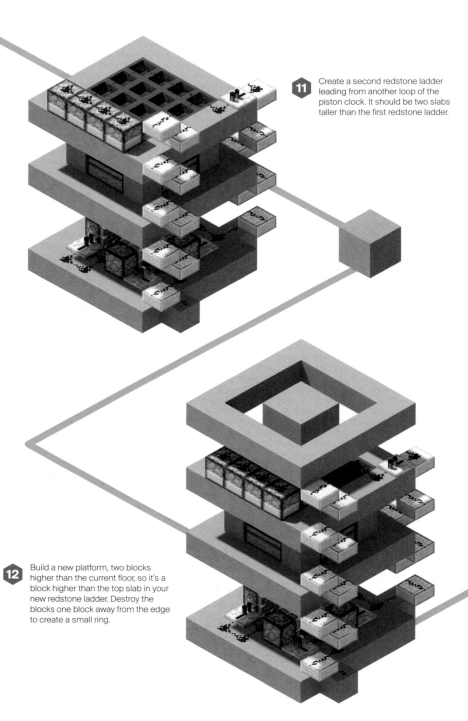

11 Create a second redstone ladder leading from another loop of the piston clock. It should be two slabs taller than the first redstone ladder.

12 Build a new platform, two blocks higher than the current floor, so it's a block higher than the top slab in your new redstone ladder. Destroy the blocks one block away from the edge to create a small ring.

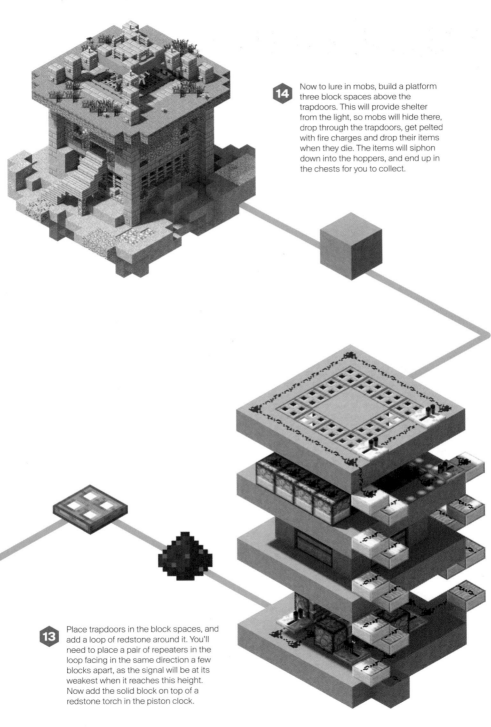

14 Now to lure in mobs, build a platform three block spaces above the trapdoors. This will provide shelter from the light, so mobs will hide there, drop through the trapdoors, get pelted with fire charges and drop their items when they die. The items will siphon down into the hoppers, and end up in the chests for you to collect.

13 Place trapdoors in the block spaces, and add a loop of redstone around it. You'll need to place a pair of repeaters in the loop facing in the same direction a few blocks apart, as the signal will be at its weakest when it reaches this height. Now add the solid block on top of a redstone torch in the piston clock.

47

PULSE CIRCUIT

The next circuit type is the pulse circuit, which focuses less on multiple triggers, and more on adapting signal duration as it travels through a circuit. This allows redstone mechanisms to stay active for a determined length of time.

PULSE CREATION

Like clock circuits, there are many different ways to create pulse circuits. However, pulse circuits are made from multiple elements, as featured here, that can be included and combined to make a truly customisable contraption.

TIP

Some pulses may be too lengthy to pass through a multiplier – they won't end before the second pulse reaches its destination. Run long pulses through a limiter first if this happens.

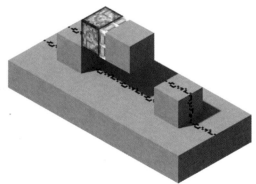

PULSE GENERATOR

All pulse circuits begin with a generator, which creates the initial pulse. In this one, a single lever controls two adjacent repeaters, one of which powers a third repeater, causing it to lock. When the lever is pulled again, the repeaters deactivate, releasing the lock on the final repeater. This in turn releases a built-up redstone pulse into a circuit.

LIMITER

The limiter reduces the length of a pulse. It raises redstone dust by one block on both sides of a three-block dip, with a sticky piston and solid block positioned above. When the pulse travels over the first raised block, the piston pushes the block and severs the redstone. When it deactivates, the redstone reattaches, allowing the reduced pulse through.

EXTENDER

This extender is highly customisable and can adapt a pulse to last hundreds of ticks! The item in the dropper is passed to the hopper and back, alternating whether the first comparator measures any storage. A pulse is then sent via a repeater, through a block, beginning the passage of items between the final hoppers. The pulse will last as long as it takes to pass all items back and forth, so you can lengthen the pulse by adding more items. Another comparator and repeater are situated between the two sets of hoppers to resupply the item to the dropper and reset the system.

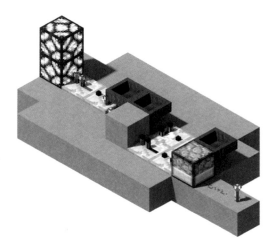

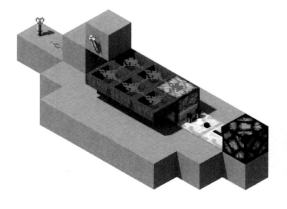

MULTIPLIER

Multipliers take a single pulse input and increase the number of pulses they emit, quickly activating a mechanism twice or more. The signal first passes through a solid block, powering the redstone lamps, and along the loop next to it, passing the signal to the comparator set to subtraction mode. It passes through the solid block once again, but won't reach the comparator as the signal strength has been reduced by the first subtraction.

COUNTER

The opposite to a multiplier, the counter emits a pulse only when it has reached the required number of pulse inputs. This counter requires six pulse inputs before it will output a signal, which it achieves by passing a single item around the hoppers in a loop, until it reaches the dropper. The comparator then detects the item and outputs a pulse. Note that the output tube of each hopper faces into the next one, and the final hopper's output tube faces into the dropper.

COMBINATION LOCK

This circuit combines generators, an extender and a counter into one simple contraption that can protect your base or storage area. It uses a wall of dummy buttons so that only people who know the right combination can enter.

YOU WILL NEED:

| 168 | 1 | 1 | 7 | 33 | 8 | 6 | 2 | 4 | 21 | 20 |

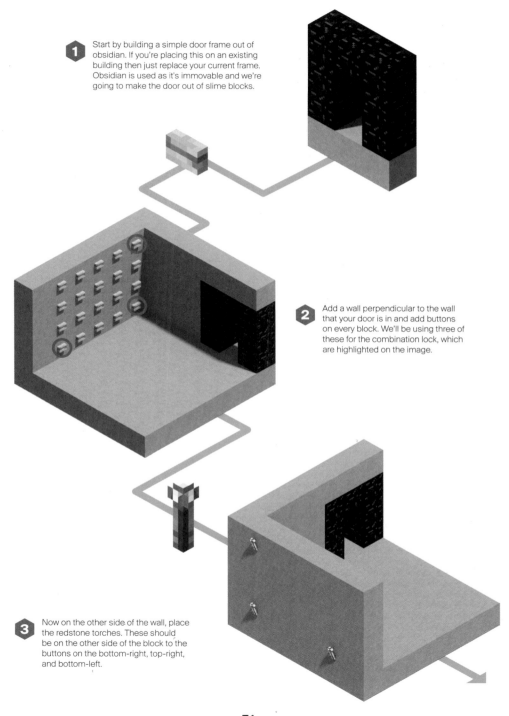

1. Start by building a simple door frame out of obsidian. If you're placing this on an existing building then just replace your current frame. Obsidian is used as it's immovable and we're going to make the door out of slime blocks.

2. Add a wall perpendicular to the wall that your door is in and add buttons on every block. We'll be using three of these for the combination lock, which are highlighted on the image.

3. Now on the other side of the wall, place the redstone torches. These should be on the other side of the block to the buttons on the bottom-right, top-right, and bottom-left.

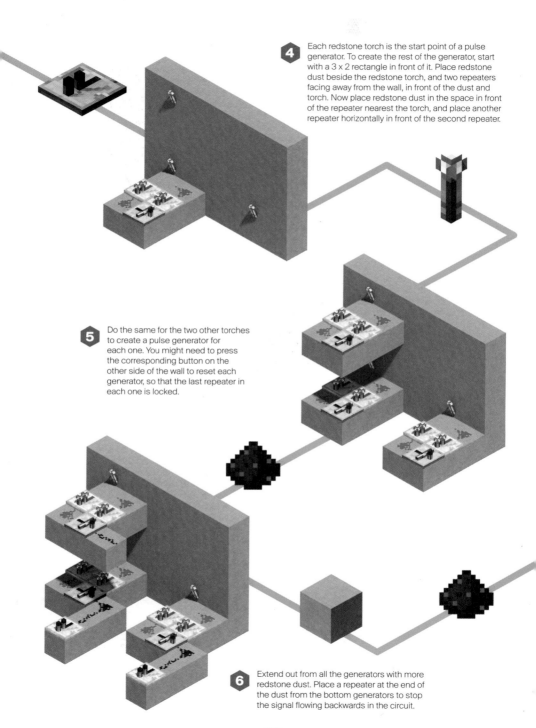

4 Each redstone torch is the start point of a pulse generator. To create the rest of the generator, start with a 3 x 2 rectangle in front of it. Place redstone dust beside the redstone torch, and two repeaters facing away from the wall, in front of the dust and torch. Now place redstone dust in the space in front of the repeater nearest the torch, and place another repeater horizontally in front of the second repeater.

5 Do the same for the two other torches to create a pulse generator for each one. You might need to press the corresponding button on the other side of the wall to reset each generator, so that the last repeater in each one is locked.

6 Extend out from all the generators with more redstone dust. Place a repeater at the end of the dust from the bottom generators to stop the signal flowing backwards in the circuit.

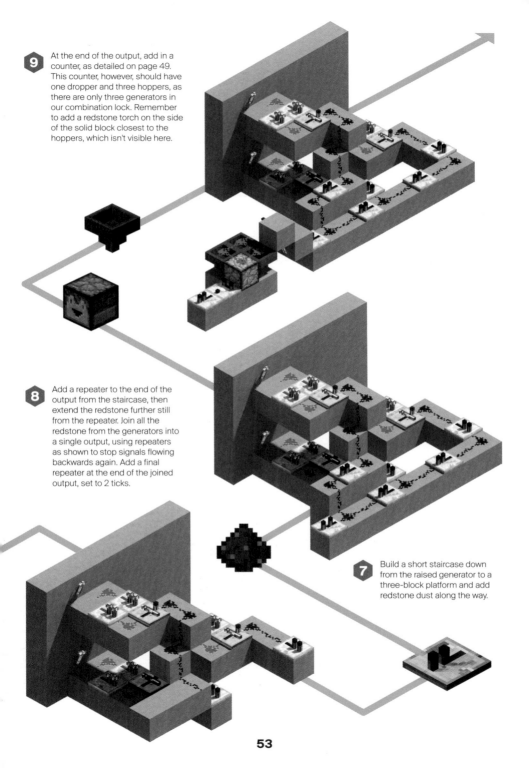

9 At the end of the output, add in a counter, as detailed on page 49. This counter, however, should have one dropper and three hoppers, as there are only three generators in our combination lock. Remember to add a redstone torch on the side of the solid block closest to the hoppers, which isn't visible here.

8 Add a repeater to the end of the output from the staircase, then extend the redstone further still from the repeater. Join all the redstone from the generators into a single output, using repeaters as shown to stop signals flowing backwards again. Add a final repeater at the end of the joined output, set to 2 ticks.

7 Build a short staircase down from the raised generator to a three-block platform and add redstone dust along the way.

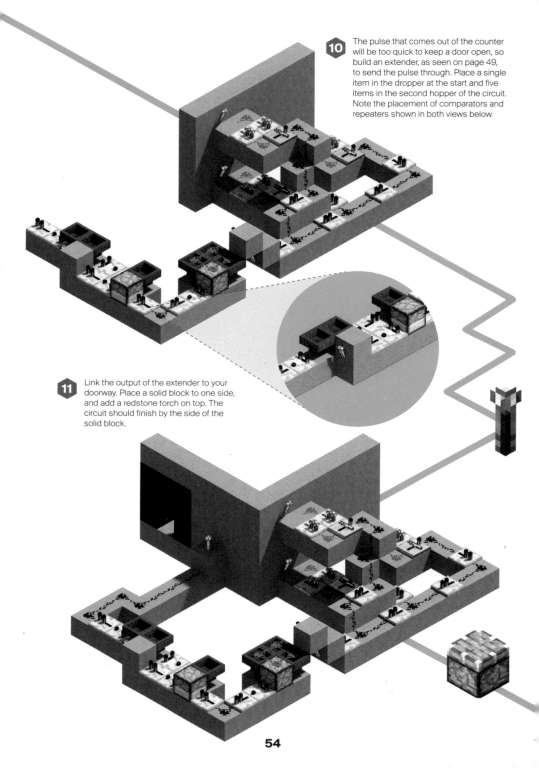

10 The pulse that comes out of the counter will be too quick to keep a door open, so build an extender, as seen on page 49, to send the pulse through. Place a single item in the dropper at the start and five items in the second hopper of the circuit. Note the placement of comparators and repeaters shown in both views below.

11 Link the output of the extender to your doorway. Place a solid block to one side, and add a redstone torch on top. The circuit should finish by the side of the solid block.

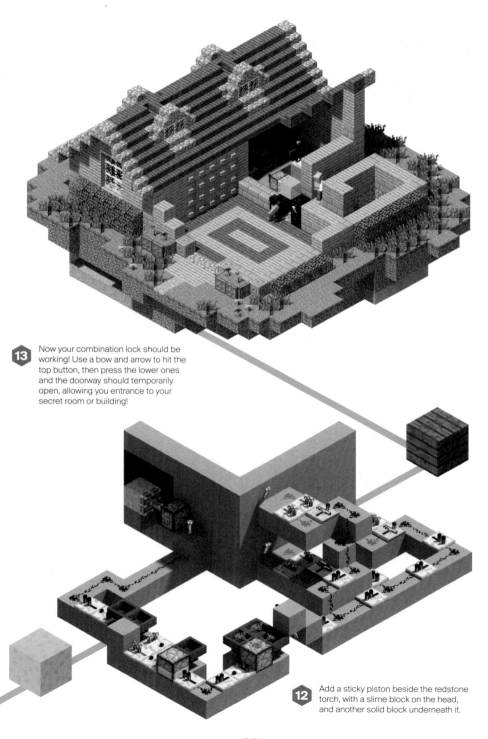

13 Now your combination lock should be working! Use a bow and arrow to hit the top button, then press the lower ones and the doorway should temporarily open, allowing you entrance to your secret room or building!

12 Add a sticky piston beside the redstone torch, with a slime block on the head, and another solid block underneath it.

VERTICAL TRANSMISSION

We've seen ways to create horizontal circuits, but often when creating redstone mechanisms, you'll need elements on different levels. Vertical transmission will enable your redstone to travel along a new third dimension.

VERTICAL CIRCUIT CREATION

Vertical transmission seems quite difficult, but is actually really easy when you know how. It can rely on the basic behaviours of redstone, or inversion of constant power sources, and can be used to send redstone signals up and down in contraptions.

TIP

This build also shows how other redstone power sources can be used to turn off the bottom redstone torch, changing the order of inversion.

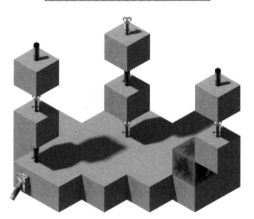

BASIC VERTICAL TRANSMISSION

The simplest way of building vertical transmission is to utilise redstone's inherent ability to join between blocks one space higher or lower. This takes up a lot of space if you're trying to create a compact build, but redstone will join up around corners travelling vertically, allowing spiral 'staircases'.

TORCH TOWER

This circuit uses inverted torches and minimal floor space to reach an elevated point. The redstone torch provides a signal through the block above, deactivating the torch on top, allowing the next torch to stay active, and so on. The necessity for pairs of redstone torches and solid blocks means it can lack precision.

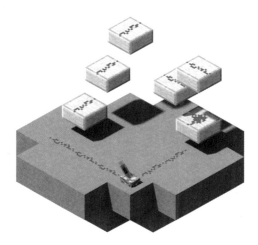

REDSTONE LADDER

Unlike full blocks, partial blocks such as slabs won't sever redstone dust if stacked in an alternating formation. This means they can be used to create ladders when placed in the top half of a block space. Other blocks that can be used to similar effect include hoppers and upside-down stairs.

STICKY PISTON TOWER

Sending signals downwards in a small space is harder to do, but still possible. This tower uses a redstone block placed on a sticky piston, facing downwards. When the block above the piston is powered, the piston extends, pushing the redstone block directly above the redstone dust, activating it in turn. This mechanism can also be stacked to pass a signal from great heights.

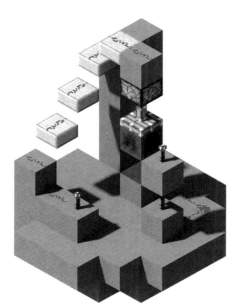

COMBINATION TRANSMISSION

Each transmission circuit has strengths and weaknesses; some take up lots of space, others will only stack at certain increments, while others still will only travel up or down. By combining the various systems, you can create unique circuits that compensate for a system's shortcomings with another's strength.

ARMOUR SWAPPER

To show vertical transmission in practice, we're going to build a clever wardrobe solution. With a few pulls of a lever, the armour swapper can cycle through your available armours, allowing you to choose one that suits your impending adventure.

YOU WILL NEED:

3	1	2	8	3	4	1	2	8	1	1

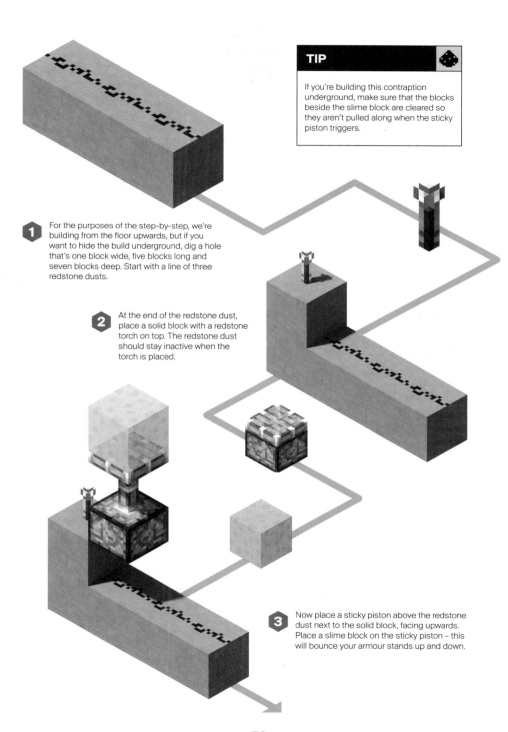

TIP

If you're building this contraption underground, make sure that the blocks beside the slime block are cleared so they aren't pulled along when the sticky piston triggers.

1 For the purposes of the step-by-step, we're building from the floor upwards, but if you want to hide the build underground, dig a hole that's one block wide, five blocks long and seven blocks deep. Start with a line of three redstone dusts.

2 At the end of the redstone dust, place a solid block with a redstone torch on top. The redstone dust should stay inactive when the torch is placed.

3 Now place a sticky piston above the redstone dust next to the solid block, facing upwards. Place a slime block on the sticky piston - this will bounce your armour stands up and down.

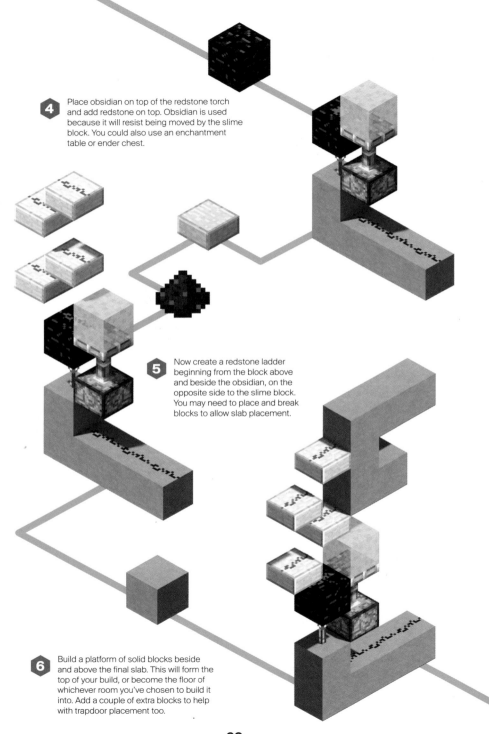

4 Place obsidian on top of the redstone torch and add redstone on top. Obsidian is used because it will resist being moved by the slime block. You could also use an enchantment table or ender chest.

5 Now create a redstone ladder beginning from the block above and beside the obsidian, on the opposite side to the slime block. You may need to place and break blocks to allow slab placement.

6 Build a platform of solid blocks beside and above the final slab. This will form the top of your build, or become the floor of whichever room you've chosen to build it into. Add a couple of extra blocks to help with trapdoor placement too.

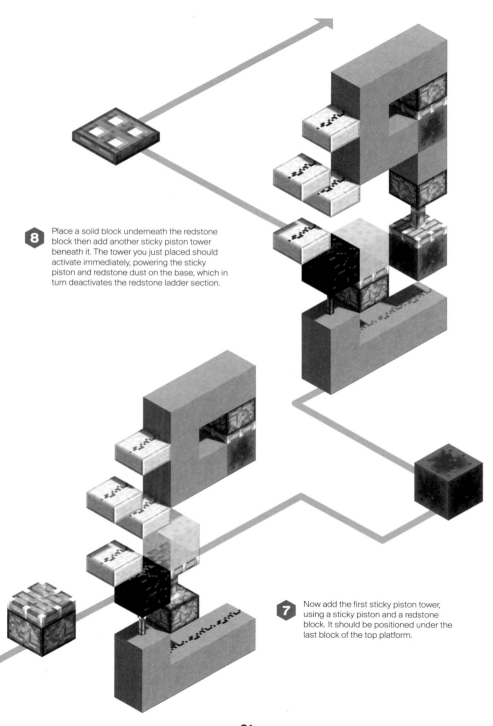

8 Place a solid block underneath the redstone block then add another sticky piston tower beneath it. The tower you just placed should activate immediately, powering the sticky piston and redstone dust on the base, which in turn deactivates the redstone ladder section.

7 Now add the first sticky piston tower, using a sticky piston and a redstone block. It should be positioned under the last block of the top platform.

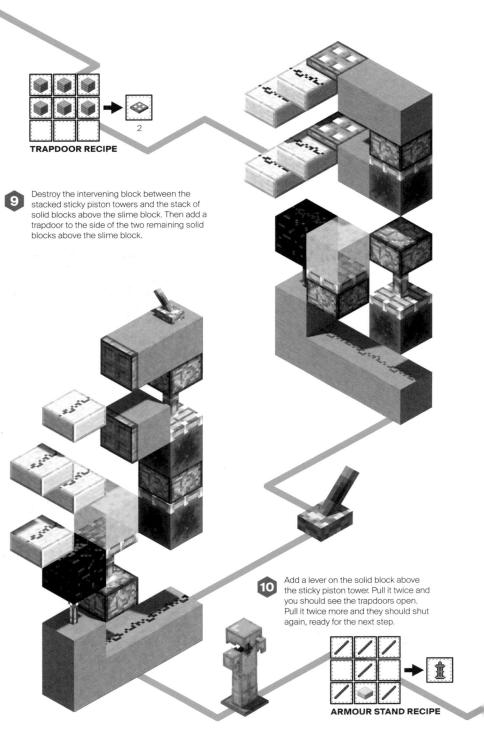

TRAPDOOR RECIPE

9 Destroy the intervening block between the stacked sticky piston towers and the stack of solid blocks above the slime block. Then add a trapdoor to the side of the two remaining solid blocks above the slime block.

10 Add a lever on the solid block above the sticky piston tower. Pull it twice and you should see the trapdoors open. Pull it twice more and they should shut again, ready for the next step.

ARMOUR STAND RECIPE

When you pull the lever, the sticky piston towers will activate in sequence, turning off the redstone dust on the base. This in turn opens both the trapdoors, and activates the piston with the slime block attached. The armour stands on the trapdoors drop, while the one on the slime block is ejected upwards. The trapdoors quickly close, alternating the position of the armour stands, allowing you to choose your favourite.

Now add the armour stands. Place one on top of the trapdoor – you will need to crouch while placing – and decorate with a set of armour. Pull the lever twice to make it disappear. Now do the same thing with two new armour stands. If it's worked correctly, you should now have your first set of armour in front of you.

3

BIG BUILDS

Now you're a redstone master, it's time to put all your
new knowledge to good use. The final section features
big projects, each of which incorporates various redstone
components and different circuits that we've learned
about in previous sections, and combines them to create
something truly incredible!

PLATFORM ELEVATOR

The first of our big builds combines observer output, vertical transmission, slime blocks and obsidian to create a clever elevator that can travel up or down, and can be summoned whether you're standing at the top of a structure or at the bottom. It's perfect for adding to tall buildings like skyscrapers.

YOU WILL NEED:

| 9 | 6 | 2 | 2 | 5 | 2 | 2 | 16 | 47 | 1 |

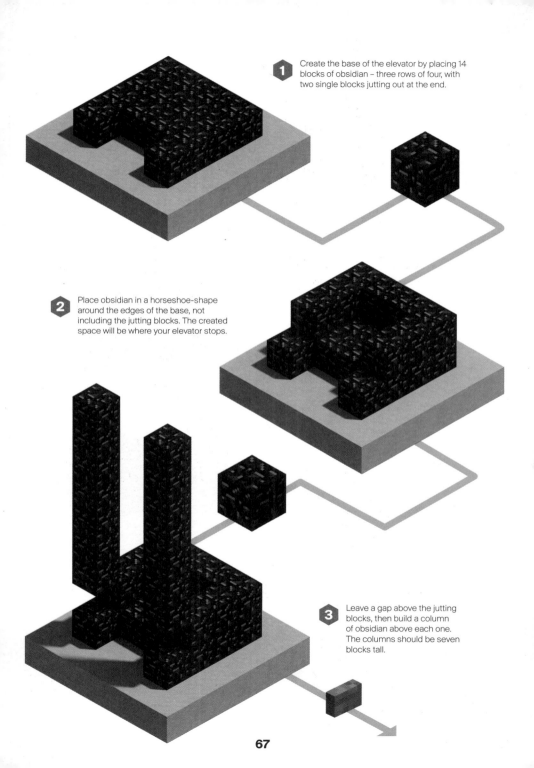

1 Create the base of the elevator by placing 14 blocks of obsidian – three rows of four, with two single blocks jutting out at the end.

2 Place obsidian in a horseshoe-shape around the edges of the base, not including the jutting blocks. The created space will be where your elevator stops.

3 Leave a gap above the jutting blocks, then build a column of obsidian above each one. The columns should be seven blocks tall.

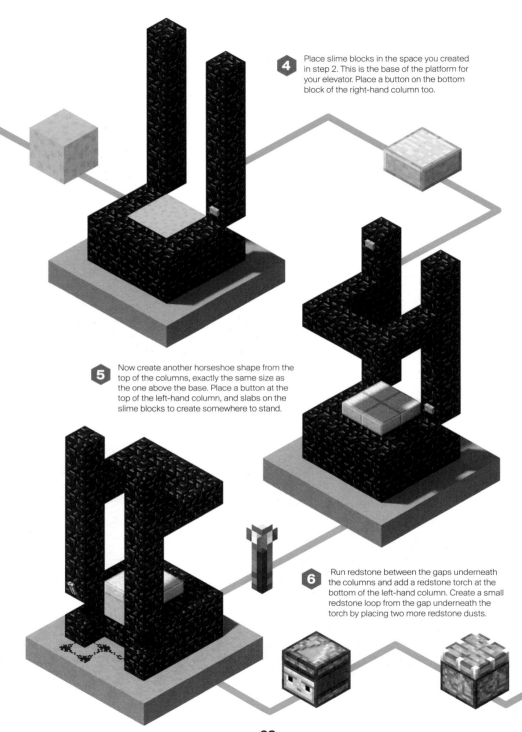

4 Place slime blocks in the space you created in step 2. This is the base of the platform for your elevator. Place a button on the bottom block of the right-hand column too.

5 Now create another horseshoe shape from the top of the columns, exactly the same size as the one above the base. Place a button at the top of the left-hand column, and slabs on the slime blocks to create somewhere to stand.

6 Run redstone between the gaps underneath the columns and add a redstone torch at the bottom of the left-hand column. Create a small redstone loop from the gap underneath the torch by placing two more redstone dusts.

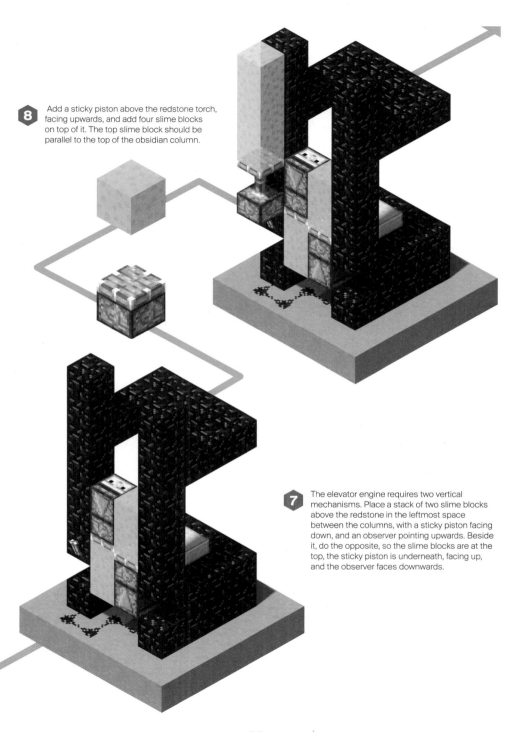

8 Add a sticky piston above the redstone torch, facing upwards, and add four slime blocks on top of it. The top slime block should be parallel to the top of the obsidian column.

7 The elevator engine requires two vertical mechanisms. Place a stack of two slime blocks above the redstone in the leftmost space between the columns, with a sticky piston facing down, and an observer pointing upwards. Beside it, do the opposite, so the slime blocks are at the top, the sticky piston is underneath, facing up, and the observer faces downwards.

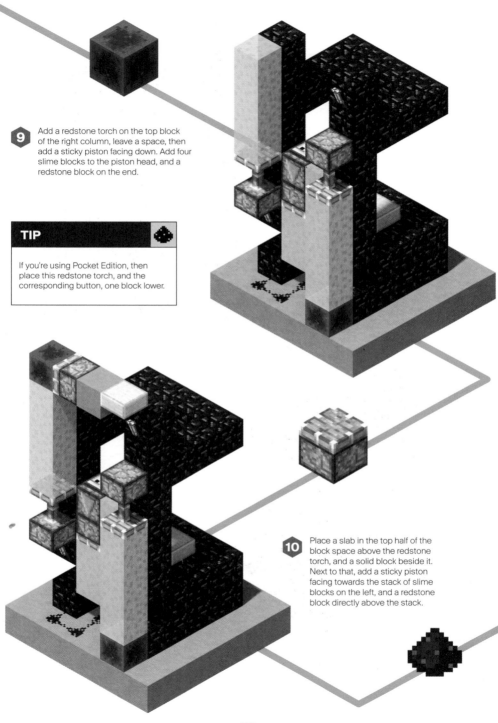

9 Add a redstone torch on the top block of the right column, leave a space, then add a sticky piston facing down. Add four slime blocks to the piston head, and a redstone block on the end.

TIP

If you're using Pocket Edition, then place this redstone torch, and the corresponding button, one block lower.

10 Place a slab in the top half of the block space above the redstone torch, and a solid block beside it. Next to that, add a sticky piston facing towards the stack of slime blocks on the left, and a redstone block directly above the stack.

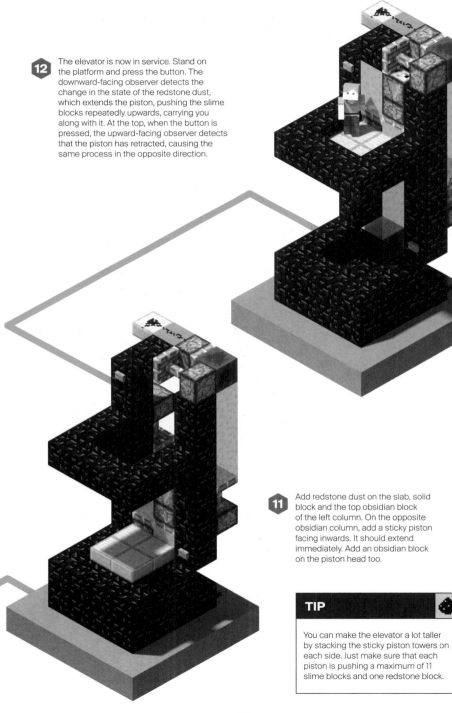

12 The elevator is now in service. Stand on the platform and press the button. The downward-facing observer detects the change in the state of the redstone dust, which extends the piston, pushing the slime blocks repeatedly upwards, carrying you along with it. At the top, when the button is pressed, the upward-facing observer detects that the piston has retracted, causing the same process in the opposite direction.

11 Add redstone dust on the slab, solid block and the top obsidian block of the left column. On the opposite obsidian column, add a sticky piston facing inwards. It should extend immediately. Add an obsidian block on the piston head too.

TIP

You can make the elevator a lot taller by stacking the sticky piston towers on each side. Just make sure that each piston is pushing a maximum of 11 slime blocks and one redstone block.

ELYTRA LAUNCHER

Gliding across the Minecraft world is one of the fastest ways to travel. This elytra launcher combines a vertical transmission circuit with slime blocks, dispensers and TNT to hurl you in the air so you can easily float to your destination.

YOU WILL NEED:

| 25 | 8 | 5 | 1 | 1 | 1 | 1 | 1 | 10 | 45 | 42 |

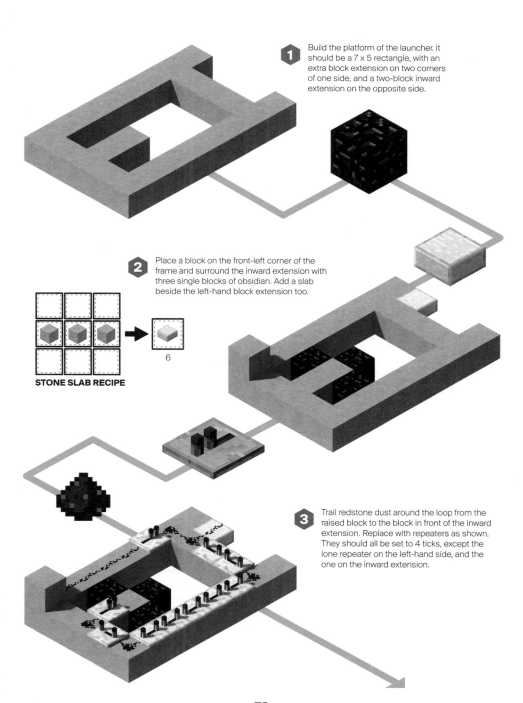

1 Build the platform of the launcher. It should be a 7 x 5 rectangle, with an extra block extension on two corners of one side, and a two-block inward extension on the opposite side.

2 Place a block on the front-left corner of the frame and surround the inward extension with three single blocks of obsidian. Add a slab beside the left-hand block extension too.

STONE SLAB RECIPE

6

3 Trail redstone dust around the loop from the raised block to the block in front of the inward extension. Replace with repeaters as shown. They should all be set to 4 ticks, except the lone repeater on the left-hand side, and the one on the inward extension.

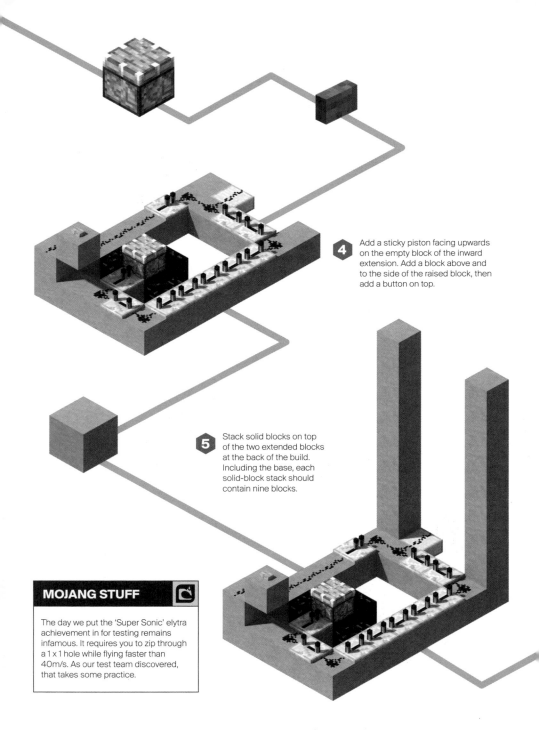

4 Add a sticky piston facing upwards on the empty block of the inward extension. Add a block above and to the side of the raised block, then add a button on top.

5 Stack solid blocks on top of the two extended blocks at the back of the build. Including the base, each solid-block stack should contain nine blocks.

MOJANG STUFF

The day we put the 'Super Sonic' elytra achievement in for testing remains infamous. It requires you to zip through a 1 x 1 hole while flying faster than 40m/s. As our test team discovered, that takes some practice.

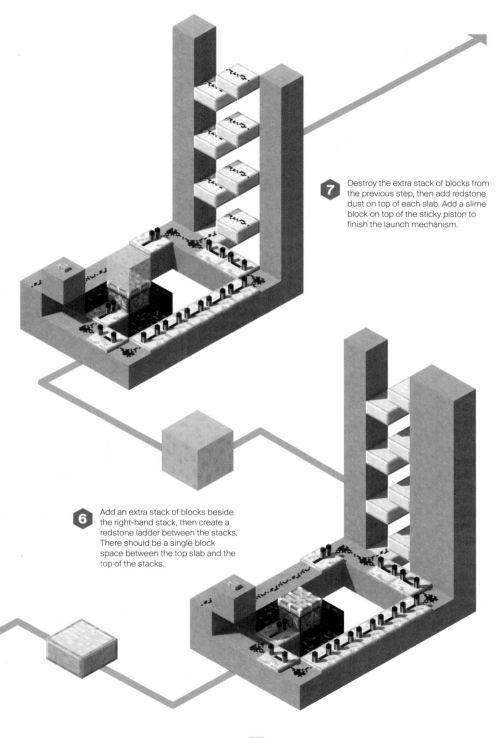

7 Destroy the extra stack of blocks from the previous step, then add redstone dust on top of each slab. Add a slime block on top of the sticky piston to finish the launch mechanism.

6 Add an extra stack of blocks beside the right-hand stack, then create a redstone ladder between the stacks. There should be a single block space between the top slab and the top of the stacks.

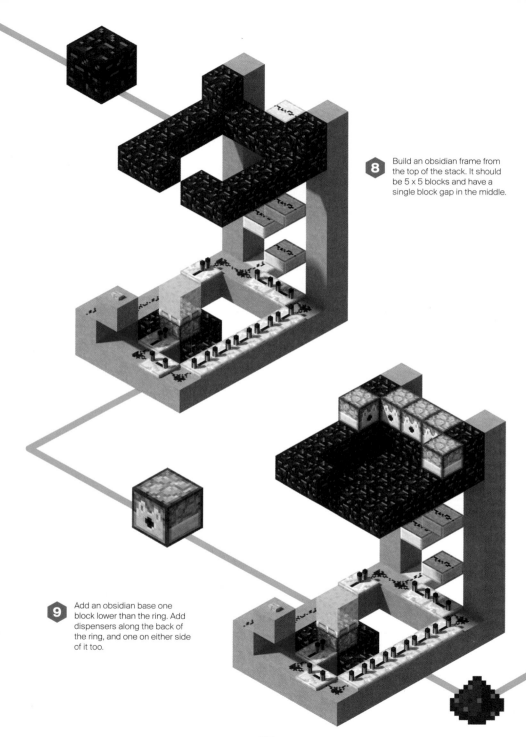

8 Build an obsidian frame from the top of the stack. It should be 5 x 5 blocks and have a single block gap in the middle.

9 Add an obsidian base one block lower than the ring. Add dispensers along the back of the ring, and one on either side of it too.

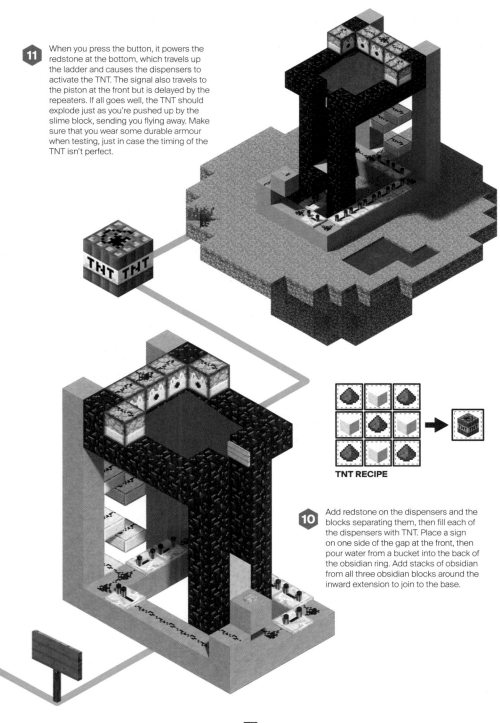

When you press the button, it powers the redstone at the bottom, which travels up the ladder and causes the dispensers to activate the TNT. The signal also travels to the piston at the front but is delayed by the repeaters. If all goes well, the TNT should explode just as you're pushed up by the slime block, sending you flying away. Make sure that you wear some durable armour when testing, just in case the timing of the TNT isn't perfect.

TNT RECIPE

Add redstone on the dispensers and the blocks separating them, then fill each of the dispensers with TNT. Place a sign on one side of the gap at the front, then pour water from a bucket into the back of the obsidian ring. Add stacks of obsidian from all three obsidian blocks around the inward extension to join to the base.

PISTON SQUISHER

An excellent example of a redstone trap, the piston squisher uses pressure plates to activate two sets of pistons, above and below, connected by a redstone tower. The result is a claustrophobic, nigh-on inescapable chamber.

YOU WILL NEED:

| 27 | 179 | 48 | 16 | 4 | 16 |

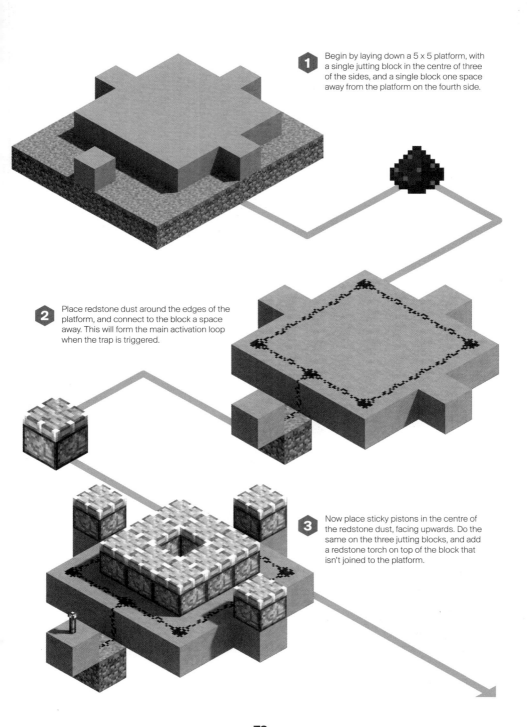

1 Begin by laying down a 5 x 5 platform, with a single jutting block in the centre of three of the sides, and a single block one space away from the platform on the fourth side.

2 Place redstone dust around the edges of the platform, and connect to the block a space away. This will form the main activation loop when the trap is triggered.

3 Now place sticky pistons in the centre of the redstone dust, facing upwards. Do the same on the three jutting blocks, and add a redstone torch on top of the block that isn't joined to the platform.

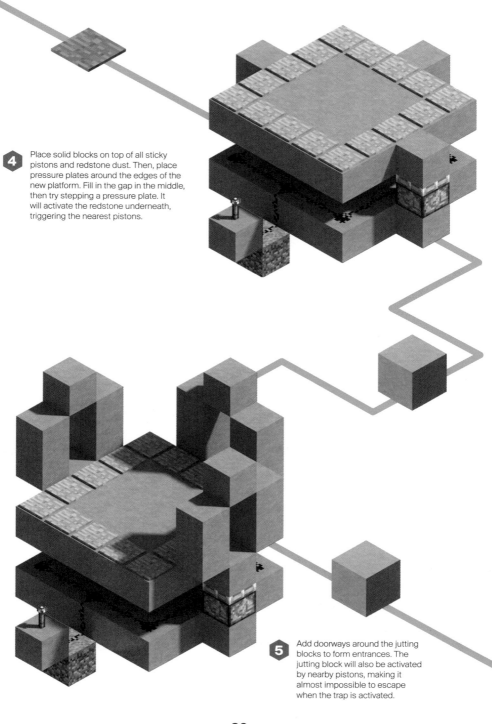

4 Place solid blocks on top of all sticky pistons and redstone dust. Then, place pressure plates around the edges of the new platform. Fill in the gap in the middle, then try stepping a pressure plate. It will activate the redstone underneath, triggering the nearest pistons.

5 Add doorways around the jutting blocks to form entrances. The jutting block will also be activated by nearby pistons, making it almost impossible to escape when the trap is activated.

80

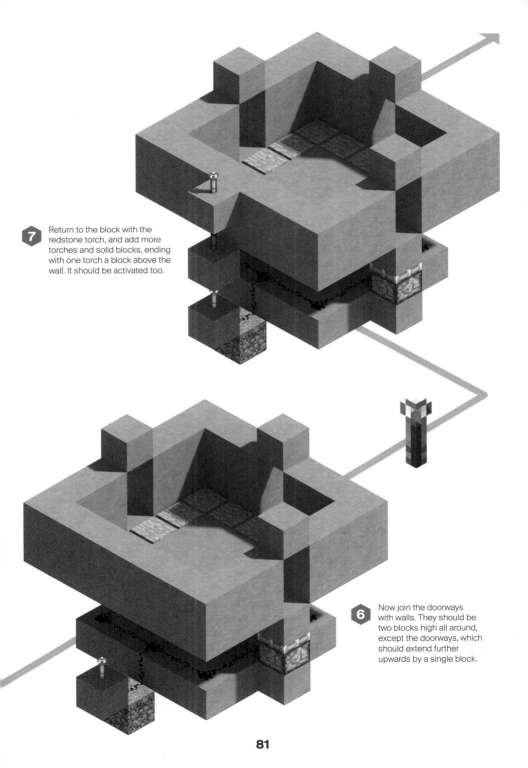

7 Return to the block with the redstone torch, and add more torches and solid blocks, ending with one torch a block above the wall. It should be activated too.

6 Now join the doorways with walls. They should be two blocks high all around, except the doorways, which should extend further upwards by a single block.

81

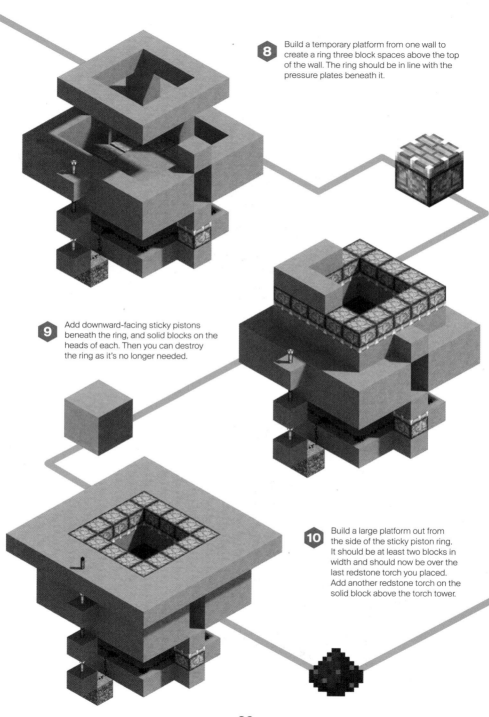

8 Build a temporary platform from one wall to create a ring three block spaces above the top of the wall. The ring should be in line with the pressure plates beneath it.

9 Add downward-facing sticky pistons beneath the ring, and solid blocks on the heads of each. Then you can destroy the ring as it's no longer needed.

10 Build a large platform out from the side of the sticky piston ring. It should be at least two blocks in width and should now be over the last redstone torch you placed. Add another redstone torch on the solid block above the torch tower.

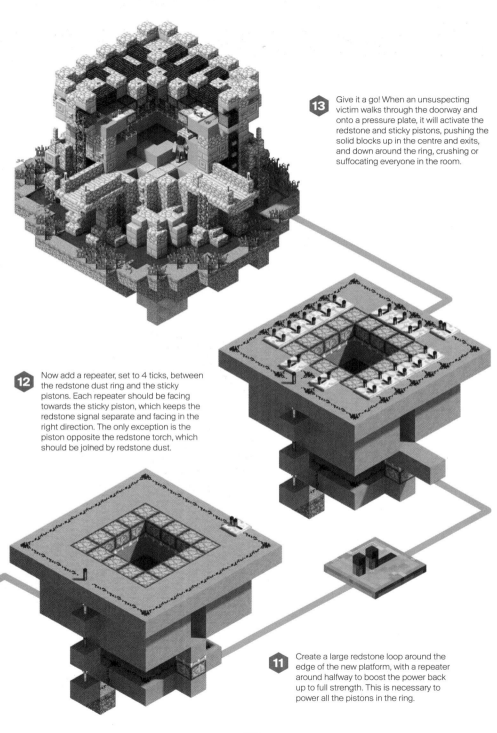

13 Give it a go! When an unsuspecting victim walks through the doorway and onto a pressure plate, it will activate the redstone and sticky pistons, pushing the solid blocks up in the centre and exits, and down around the ring, crushing or suffocating everyone in the room.

12 Now add a repeater, set to 4 ticks, between the redstone dust ring and the sticky pistons. Each repeater should be facing towards the sticky piston, which keeps the redstone signal separate and facing in the right direction. The only exception is the piston opposite the redstone torch, which should be joined by redstone dust.

11 Create a large redstone loop around the edge of the new platform, with a repeater around halfway to boost the power back up to full strength. This is necessary to power all the pistons in the ring.

AUTOMATIC BREWER

Brewing potions is very handy, but can be a nightmare if you need to collect dozens of ingredients. This handy redstone workshop uses dispensers to gather the necessary items and automatically feed them into a brewing stand, taking the work out of brewing.

YOU WILL NEED:

| 3 | 8 | 4 | 1 | 2 | 17 | 2 | 14 | 15 | 11 | 7 |

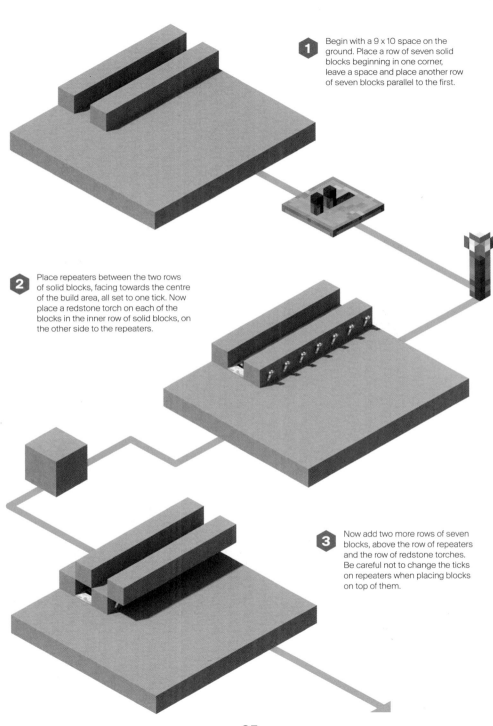

1 Begin with a 9 x 10 space on the ground. Place a row of seven solid blocks beginning in one corner, leave a space and place another row of seven blocks parallel to the first.

2 Place repeaters between the two rows of solid blocks, facing towards the centre of the build area, all set to one tick. Now place a redstone torch on each of the blocks in the inner row of solid blocks, on the other side to the repeaters.

3 Now add two more rows of seven blocks, above the row of repeaters and the row of redstone torches. Be careful not to change the ticks on repeaters when placing blocks on top of them.

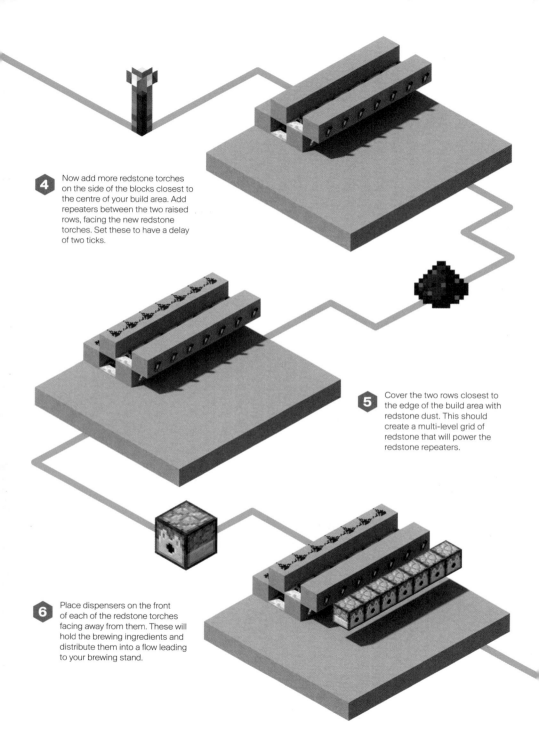

4 Now add more redstone torches on the side of the blocks closest to the centre of your build area. Add repeaters between the two raised rows, facing the new redstone torches. Set these to have a delay of two ticks.

5 Cover the two rows closest to the edge of the build area with redstone dust. This should create a multi-level grid of redstone that will power the redstone repeaters.

6 Place dispensers on the front of each of the redstone torches facing away from them. These will hold the brewing ingredients and distribute them into a flow leading to your brewing stand.

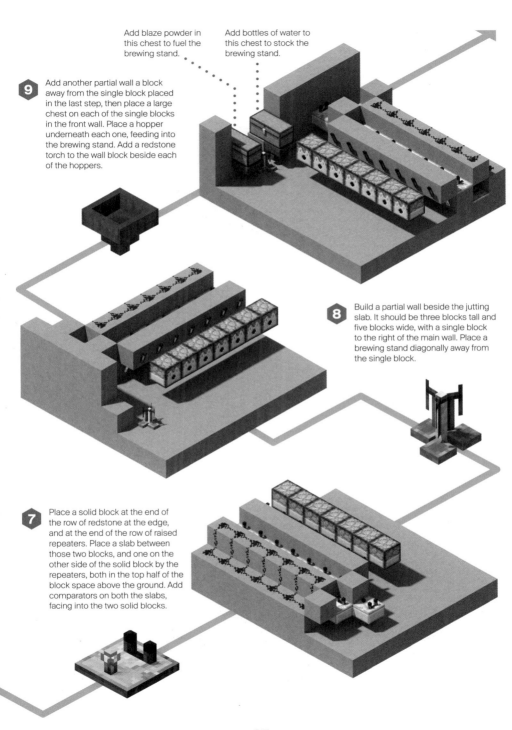

Add blaze powder in this chest to fuel the brewing stand.

Add bottles of water to this chest to stock the brewing stand.

9 Add another partial wall a block away from the single block placed in the last step, then place a large chest on each of the single blocks in the front wall. Place a hopper underneath each one, feeding into the brewing stand. Add a redstone torch to the wall block beside each of the hoppers.

8 Build a partial wall beside the jutting slab. It should be three blocks tall and five blocks wide, with a single block to the right of the main wall. Place a brewing stand diagonally away from the single block.

7 Place a solid block at the end of the row of redstone at the edge, and at the end of the row of raised repeaters. Place a slab between those two blocks, and one on the other side of the solid block by the repeaters, both in the top half of the block space above the ground. Add comparators on both the slabs, facing into the two solid blocks.

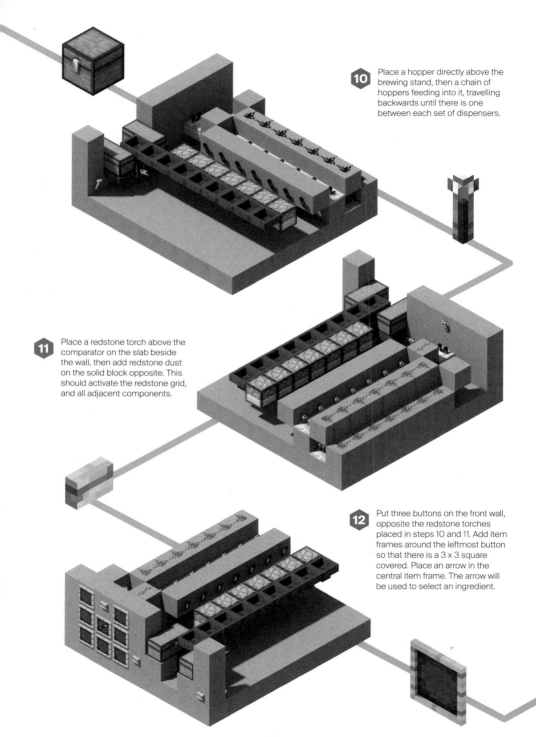

10 Place a hopper directly above the brewing stand, then a chain of hoppers feeding into it, travelling backwards until there is one between each set of dispensers.

11 Place a redstone torch above the comparator on the slab beside the wall, then add redstone dust on the solid block opposite. This should activate the redstone grid, and all adjacent components.

12 Put three buttons on the front wall, opposite the redstone torches placed in steps 10 and 11. Add item frames around the leftmost button so that there is a 3 x 3 square covered. Place an arrow in the central item frame. The arrow will be used to select an ingredient.

14 Now you're ready! Press each of the buttons either side of the brewing stand to fill with bottles of water and fuel with blaze powder. Now rotate the arrow until it is pointing at the item you want to add. The comparator on the other side of the frame will detect the direction of the item in the frame and produce a varying signal, powering the correct dispenser, which passes the ingredient down the hoppers and into the brewing stand.

TIP

In this build the comparator detects the direction of the arrow in the item frame. Comparators can also detect how many pieces of a cake are left, which record is playing on a jukebox, or whether an end portal frame block contains an eye of ender.

13 Place an ingredient on each of the item frames, then stock the corresponding dispenser with stacks of the item. Refer to the numbering for an indication of which position will activate each dispenser.

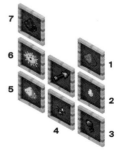

1 - GUNPOWDER	5 - GLOWSTONE DUST
2 - GHAST TEAR	6 - PUFFERFISH
3 - SPIDER EYE	7 - REDSTONE DUST
4 - NETHER WART	

REDSTONE LIGHTHOUSE

For the final build, we're going to combine a simple torch clock with vertical transmission to make a grand lighthouse, visible from miles around. It's the perfect mechanism to mark your territory and light the way for visitors.

YOU WILL NEED:

24	54	5	12	97

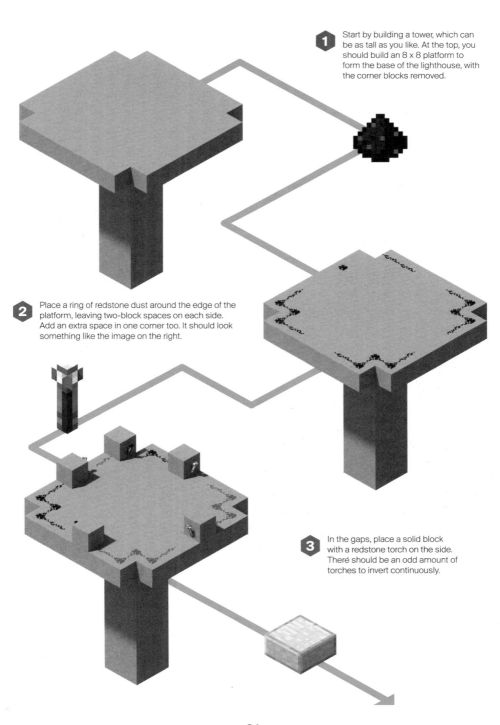

1. Start by building a tower, which can be as tall as you like. At the top, you should build an 8 x 8 platform to form the base of the lighthouse, with the corner blocks removed.

2. Place a ring of redstone dust around the edge of the platform, leaving two-block spaces on each side. Add an extra space in one corner too. It should look something like the image on the right.

3. In the gaps, place a solid block with a redstone torch on the side. Theré should be an odd amount of torches to invert continuously.

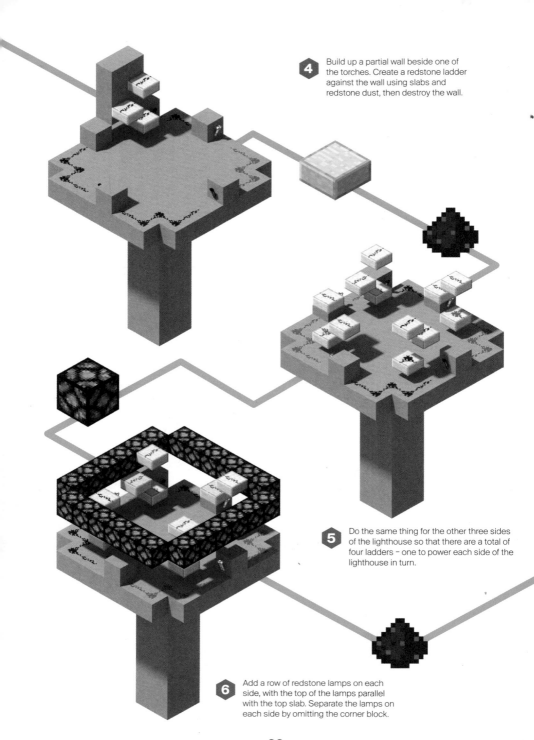

4 Build up a partial wall beside one of the torches. Create a redstone ladder against the wall using slabs and redstone dust, then destroy the wall.

5 Do the same thing for the other three sides of the lighthouse so that there are a total of four ladders – one to power each side of the lighthouse in turn.

6 Add a row of redstone lamps on each side, with the top of the lamps parallel with the top slab. Separate the lamps on each side by omitting the corner block.

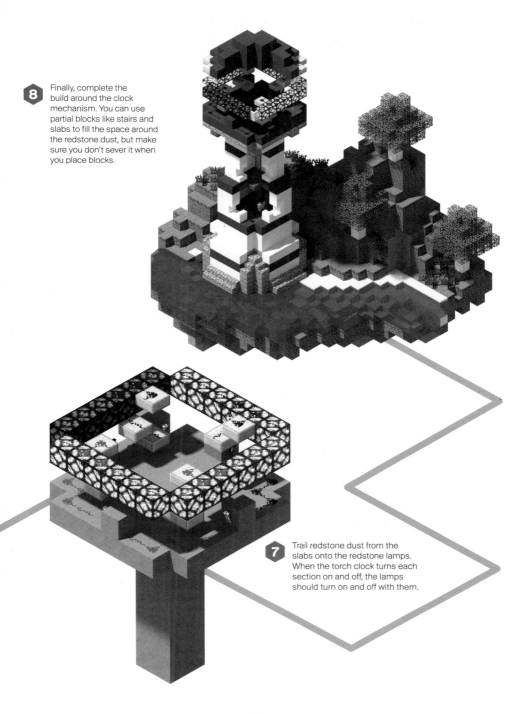

8 Finally, complete the build around the clock mechanism. You can use partial blocks like stairs and slabs to fill the space around the redstone dust, but make sure you don't sever it when you place blocks.

7 Trail redstone dust from the slabs onto the redstone lamps. When the torch clock turns each section on and off, the lamps should turn on and off with them.

FINAL WORDS

Phew! You made it. Hopefully you can now tell your comparators from your repeaters, pulse circuits from clock circuits and how to fix up an effective hopper, dropper or swapper. With any luck, you can combine this elite wisdom to assemble devices capable of the most devious computation, propelling players to new heights, or setting imaginations (and mobs) alight.

The choice is yours and the possibilities are wide open. What will you build? We can't wait to see!

MARSH DAVIES
THE MOJANG TEAM

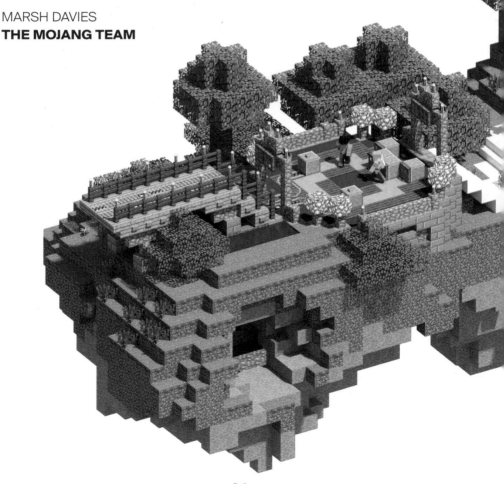